Following Jesus

BEYOND TRADITIONAL CHRISTIANITY

For modern minded individuals who seek to add depth and direction to their lives

ISBN: 1495964655
ISBN 13: 9781495964657
Library of Congress Control Number: 2014903307
CreateSpace Independent Publishing Platform
North Charleston, South Carolina

Acknowledgements

I believe I should begin this list with Tennyson's, *"I am a part of all that I have met."* Every person I have known well enough to remember a name or a face has, in some way shaped my understanding of myself, and life in general. Most I have encountered were people of decent intelligence and integrity. Their views of life – of God – of religion helped to expand my own – even when I disagreed.

Those who actually assisted in the writing of this also are numerous. My Monday morning breakfast buddies, Jim Karlak and Don Scott, reviewed sections of the manuscript and offered helpful suggestions and encouragement. Members of the Seekers class volunteered to read the manuscript as part of a class project. Their questions, comments, criticisms and observations also were extremely useful. My daughter, Dr. Cynthia Beamer, helped me focus the writing for my reader and also offered strong encouragement. My granddaughter, Kate Beamer did some very helpful editorial work. Her perspective and keen eye were essential to this finding its way into print. As with anything I have written, I give credit to my wife, Diane. Her loving encouragement, insightful comments and critical eye have been an essential part of any offering I have created.

Finally, as strange as it might seem, I want to thank my unconscious self who started and guided me through this project. In an extremely vivid dream, I was given the title and told to write this book. I spent the next year trying to organize what I knew into something that would be readable, logical and adequate. During that time and the period of writing, I frequently was awakened in the night, and prodded to write what had slipped into my conscious mind in a time of twilight sleep (Section 3 should make this thought clearer). Throughout the process I was reminded of Herman Melville's observation that "taking a book off the brain is akin to the ticklish and dangerous business of taking an old painting off a panel – you have to scrape the whole brain in order to get at it with due safety and even then, the painting may not be worth the trouble."

For me, it was rewarding to organize what I have gleaned along life's path, so that I, at least, might understand it more clearly. No book however, is complete until someone reads it, so I thank you, the reader, for making it "worth the trouble."

March 31, 2014
San Antonio, Texas

Table of Contents

PROLOGUE

WHO IS THIS AUTHOR AND WHY SHOULD YOU READ HIS WORKS?

I write this book with a blending of nostalgia and hope. I feel a profound sense of melancholy in knowing the faith of my childhood has slipped from my grasp. Yet, I simply find it impossible to accept many of the claims of that simple faith. My understanding of the world has changed to the extent that those old teachings no longer make sense to me. Also, the message that faith proclaims no longer seems important to me or to the world in which I now reside. I have many friends who still find that expression of the faith to offer a meaningful path they can follow on their spiritual journey. It guides and empowers them in worthy ways. A part of me envies them, yet I realize there is no going back. Some of my fondest memories have their roots in the churches that proclaimed that faith. Diane and I were married there with the traditional words. My children were baptized and married in those churches. Most of my greatest friendships were formed in the congregations that proclaimed that simple, traditional faith. It pains me to see so many who found themselves in my predicament and responded by ceasing their spiritual journey. They simply abandoned the Church of their childhood, no longer nurturing the seeds of faith that had been planted within them. Their time now is filled with activities which may be interesting and worthy but offer no nurture of the spirit, no help with answering some ultimate questions of life, and no meaningful avenues of sharing God's love with others.

I had little interest in formal religion in my youth and early adulthood. I experienced an extraordinary call to the ministry when I was about thirty.

Even then, as I entered into the professional ministry, I had a sense that the church was not doing that for which Jesus Christ gave his life. I could not put my finger on it, but it did not seem to be a means for changing the minds and hearts of those who were members. By and large, most members I knew were decent people. They just were not perceptibly different from some nice people I knew who did not attend any church. The more deeply I became involved, the more certain was my belief that the church must have lost its way somewhere between that first Pentecost and the present time. I decided to remain in seminary to do doctoral work in church history to see what went wrong. My reasoning was simple: in order to help the church find its way I had to understand how and why it lost it. My specialty was the Patristic period (first 400 years) and the Reformation. Those were the eras in which many doctrines were developed and, unfortunately, "written in stone."

My experience of ministry was rich and rewarding for me. I would not want to have a different life. Every congregation taught me something of value, and generated lasting, loving friendships. Yet, throughout those years I often agonized at the manner in which the Christian Church behaved and presented itself to the world. I have watched the position of clergy slip from one of respect to far less than that. I have heard sermons that insulted my intelligence. I have heard some that insulted my ethical sensibilities, for they seem to confuse economical and political philosophies with theology. I have observed the faces of congregants during sermons and have seen tired, bored faces. Far too many times I have heard what I believe to be psychologically harmful messages being spouted to people who came to hear Good News. I have observed the slippage in membership – sadly watching earnest young people abandoning the search for a life grounded in a worthy spiritual quality. There are many Christian congregations where Good News is proclaimed and people are challenged and empowered to live in joyful service to one another. However, they are more difficult to find and receive little recognition.

When I was eighteen years of age a neighbor asked me what I wanted to do to earn a livelihood. I responded that I wanted to be a writer. She smiled at me and inquired gently, "Dick what on earth do you have to write about?"

More than sixty years later, I believe I can answer her question. During my active ministry there were sermons to write and classes to teach. There was no time to write an entire book. Now in the reflective years there has been time to sort through the knowledge acquired, tested and digested, the lessons learned and the pieces of wisdom gleaned along the way. *Please understand that I am not attempting to change anyone's faith or system of faith.* Rather, I am hoping to provide those who are seeking new understandings and expressions of their faith the freedom and some tools for doing so. I do not claim any of these ideas are original. I am sure that others have stated most of them long before I thought them. I just wish to add my voice to many. Perhaps it is because I subscribe to the theory that it is better to light one small candle than to sit quietly cursing the darkness. It is my belief that when enough voices are raised and heard there will be a spiritual rebirth within our nation. This new birth will not be trying to save souls from the wrath of God. It will empower and liberate people to become genuine followers of the Man of Galilee. Their mission and message will be a modern day rephrasing of the concern for the poor and outcast, the hungry and homeless, and the children – all of our *children.* They will strive to be good ambassadors reconciling the world to one another and to our common loving Creator God. They will care for this tiny, vulnerable planet Earth and all of its inhabitants. This may be more of a dream than a reality, but I invite you now to read and dream along with me.

INTRODUCTION

Gods die when people stop believing in them. The gods of ancient Rome did not die from a virus. They merely ceased to exist from non-belief. The world had changed and they no longer held meaning for their once-faithful followers. The "God is Dead" movement in the 1960's heralded the demise of traditional Christianity in America. The form of religion that dominated the Western world from the 4th century is becoming increasingly meaningless to the average American, particularly many who are educated, progressive thinking and attempting to live fully in the contemporary world. They have moved well beyond the old paradigm of a deity who knows if you have been naughty or nice and then rewards or punishes human behavior based on that knowledge. Their psyches no longer resonate to the formula of a sinful nature requiring salvation through the sacrifice of a sin-free savior. These contemporary-oriented, thoughtful spiritual pilgrims no longer wish to be recycled sinners, constantly needing to confess sins and be temporarily washed clean, only to repeat and repeat the process endlessly.

Gods do not die quickly or easily. Paradigm paralysis is a reality. There always have been faithful believers who either will deny or fail to recognize the paradigm shift that is occurring. They will fiercely defend the old gods – the old ways. They will construct walls to keep out new understandings that may threaten the beliefs of the faithful. They will attack the new expressions of faith that encroach upon their territory. At the same time, they will agonize over the loss of faith of the younger generation, and try desperately to draw them back. The current trend is to use "contemporary" music in what they call a "Praise Service." I fear that is akin to putting oatmeal in a brand new package and then trying to sell it as "New and Improved." There always will be those who cling to the old ways for security, never bothering – or daring

– to examine them. "Give me that old time religion; it's good enough for me," has been the battle hymn for many during the nearly two thousand years of church history. I assure you, the Christian Church of today bears little resemblance to the church of the 1st century. As a practical matter it more nearly reflects the thinking of later theologians than it does that of Jesus or Simon Peter. Mainline churches are slowly but surely fading away. Some of the old mainline congregations have lost dramatic numbers. A survey that covered the period from 1960 to 2000 revealed that the United Church of Christ lost 35 percent of its membership; the Church of Christ lost 30 percent; the United Methodist Church lost 23 percent of its American membership; and the Presbyterian Church lost 21 percent. Some churches showed gains during that period, but since then have begun to decline. The severity of these losses is disguised by the normal reporting process. It is true that the decline from the merger of the Methodist Church and the Evangelical United Brethren Church to form the United Methodist Church in 1968 has been disturbing. However, if you consider that during the same time the population of the nation has increased from 179 million to 281 million, or approximately 60% you have a far more severe problem. In order to have remained stable in their representation of the national population they should have increased by 60% to 15.5 million members: not decreased to 7.7 million. The effective loss of membership in the UMC actually is slightly more than 50%, not 23%. The younger generations simply are not continuing in the tradition of their parents. If you look at the demographics you will see that within the next two decades about half of those constituting the present church will have passed their eightieth birthdays.

It is my belief that the "Old Line Churches" are fading because they do not have a message that rings true and speaks to the personal lives of the younger generations who live totally within the new paradigm. Only those who either remain in the old paradigm or are willing to bear the theology for social reasons are slowing the decline. I hasten to say that there are many who still find the old paradigm meaningful. Through it they have found a relationship with God-in-Christ.[1] This relationship guides them and empowers

1 God-in-Christ is a term I use to speak of the divine element residing in Christ that manifests all the traits of God we humans are capable of comprehending.

them, and their personal spiritual journey is rich and rewarding. The drive for justice, equality, mercy, compassion and unity has been deeply embedded in their souls. This book is not for them. Rather, it is for those who feel drawn to the Man of Galilee known as Jesus Christ, but find little of value in those churches still espousing the old paradigm.[2]

That which began as a liberating, vital spiritual movement nearly two thousand years ago has, in too many instances, deteriorated into a confining, legalistic institutionalized religion.

People seem more concerned with being the moral/ethical standard bearers and judges of society than in serving as spiritual guides and the "Body-of-Christ" ministering to a broken world. The churches that attract those who do not feel comfortable with shades of grey, but desire clear black/white boundaries and the security of knowing they are "saved" continue to grow or at least to "hold on." Others, that offer special rewards for the faithful also continue to attract those whose faith seeks to gain something for themselves. However, this is not what the original Christian faith sought to express: Jesus proclaimed, "Whoever seeks to keep his life will lose it and whoever loses his life will keep it." (Luke 17:33) Jesus' call was not to a comfortable security or special privileges, but to self-sacrifice and a perilous journey for those who dared to follow him. Eric Fromm, in his book *To Have or to Be*, published in 1976, asserted that people make an unconscious choice to live either in the *having* mode or in the *becoming* mode. The having mode is security oriented. It needs to possess certainty. This includes holding fast to formulae that offer emotional security. Those in the becoming mode are willing to abandon whatever security binds them in order to become what they believe God calls them to be. The differences are profound! As the early church became acceptable and even socially desirable in the fourth century it began to attract the very people who fled in fear from it in earlier, difficult times. Eventually those security-led people dominated it – in both leadership and as participants. Also, with the establishment of Christianity as the official religion of the land by Constantine, leadership in the church became a position of power. As a result it became attractive to people who sought power, rather than

2 Paradigm is the World View that structures a society. It establishes the nature of the world and is the setting and plot for the drama of life we act out on its stage.

those drawn by a desire to serve and who were willing to make sacrifices. In the process the Church lost its vitality and sense of purpose.[3]

The purpose of the early Christian community was to draw people into a vital, liberating relationship with God-in-Christ. Many are drawn by this into a relationship with the infinite God who, by definition, can never be fully known by finite humans. For me, Jesus Christ is the channel by which we humans discover the nature of God to enter into relations with the One Jesus called Father. Some seekers, however, have been taught to think of Jesus as God in human form, rather than as the person who fully reveals God to humanity.

As a result, they worship Jesus as God although this is contrary to all Gospel accounts.[4] Unless one wishes to have a greater god and a lesser god this either refutes the claim of theologians that Jesus was actually God-in-the-flesh or it negates the authority of Scripture. In Luke 22:42, as Jesus prays in the Garden of Gethsemane he says, "Nevertheless, Thy will, not mine, be done." This definitely declares that Jesus was quite aware that God was both different and greater than himself. The process by which Jesus was elevated in the minds of good people from *Anointed One of God* to *God Himself* will be explained in a later section.

Jesus, the Man of Galilee, sought to free the Jews of the shackles that had grown from the Torah. The original meaning of Torah was *teaching, instruction, the path or the way.* Over time, it came to mean *Law.* What once had been offered as a way of life became a legalistic requirement. The prophet Jeremiah had told the people being sent into exile that this was their punishment for having broken their covenant with God (Jeremiah 11:1-8). The Pharisees, fearing that the covenant might again be broken, tightened the boundaries and insisted upon strict enforcement of what now was *The Law.* This pattern soon was emulated in the Christian Church. Early Christians were called "People of the Way," but this was eventually replaced by those living under Papal Law. This, incidentally, was the Pharisee's great concern for the actions of Jesus. They feared he was leading the people astray, encouraging

---

3 This does not suggest there are not a great many professional clergy with servant hearts.

4 The Gospel of John that defines Jesus as the Word incarnate still has Jesus himself clearly state: "The Father is greater than I." (John 14:28)

them to ignore the law that was an essential part of the covenant. Actually, Jesus realized that what once had been a rule by which to live in a lovingly obedient relationship with God had become fearful and restrictive. His proclamations of "You have heard it said, but I say to you," found in the Sermon on the Mount in Matthew, actually was his attempt to fulfill the demands of God by pointing to the underlying principles that had given it form, thereby freeing people from the outdated legalistic interpretations. An "eye for an eye," for example, never was intended to promote revenge. It was the best that could be hoped for at the time of Moses in stopping the endless blood feuds that developed from a single act. The purpose was to establish peace as quickly as possible by requiring a punishment equal to the offense. Jesus understood that. Unfortunately, far too many who professed to worship the God of Jesus still did not get it. Many translations of the Gospel of John state that the light had come into the world but the darkness could not overcome it. Actually, that translation says something about the translators. A more literal translation is that the darkness could not *grasp* it. Some pious translator took that to mean the darkness could not overcome the light, but it actually meant just what it said: the darkness could not grasp – or *get* – it. Nicodemus did not *get it* (John 3:1-12). Jesus' brothers did not get it (John 7:5). The citizens of Jerusalem did not get it (John 10:31-39). It is obvious throughout John's gospel that the Pharisees did not get it. The high priest also did not get it (John 18: 19-24). The proper translation sets the tone for the entire Gospel and the reader can see that time and time again the people did not *get* Jesus. They were not tuned in on his wavelength and could not comprehend what he was saying. Unfortunately, this "not getting it" occurs anytime a new paradigm is presented to people who are locked into their old, comfortable way of thinking.

It is this "not getting it" coupled with the biased translations, misinterpretations, and accommodations to the culture that has distorted and dissipated the original purpose and vitality of the faith of Jesus. However, the signs of a new, redemptive and empowering paradigm – consistent with Scripture – are beginning to replace the outdated, confining paradigm of sin, guilt and heaven and hell. The new paradigm is liberating and empowering. It emphasizes the good that is inherent in humanity, not the bad or evil. It does not offer some future reward for proper belief, but assists and empowers people to live more fully as followers of Jesus in daily life. John 10:10 expresses Jesus' intent quite clearly: *"I came that you might have life abundant."* This does not suggest life eternal, but life in all of its fullness. The abundant life is free of unnecessary restrictions on one's thoughts and actions. The abundant life is free to explore new possibilities, to discover, nurture and use all the gifts that have been placed within you in worthy and useful ways. The genuinely abundant life does not define success by what one accumulates but by what a person *becomes*. Those churches that have incorporated the emerging paradigm to offer the abundant life here and now, are the ones that are growing and thriving today. They are the ones being referred to as parts of "The Emerging Church."

I invite you, the reader, to work along with me as I offer my understanding of how the Christian Church has lost its way, and propose a means by which we as individuals may work out our own salvation with less fear and trembling. As I share pieces of my journey I will share much of the Scripture, which when interpreted in light of the new paradigm will help you understand my path, and give guidance for you to find and follow your own. I will also debunk some precious beliefs about Scripture and some doctrines that I believe have misguided us. To do this, I ask you to think theologically. This requires developing a different perspective on life and requires hard work. To think theologically is to think beyond the five senses. It is to ponder the underlying meaning of the events experienced. It is to view human existence as an expression of a far greater power and vision than we can begin to grasp. To think theologically is to look beyond ourselves for an understanding of our being. Ultimately it is to ask The God Question. To think theologically is to do more than utilize catch phrases and echo accepted teachings.[5] It requires effort. It is hard work. I find that when I have been involved in working my way through a labyrinth of intricate thought I require a shower as though I had spent the time at a gym.

To think theologically demands you to be willing to challenge old, comfortable ideas about God to see whether there actually is a basis for believing them. I will give one example:

---

5 I call this *God Talk*.

Most of us have heard, and perhaps even said that, "God never gives us more than we can handle." This is a comfortable thought, designed to give encouragement to people going through difficult times. When my mind bothers to consider whether this statement is true, however, I immediately ask, "Why, then, are there so many suicides?" Common sense must at least suggest that those tortured souls who take their own lives at least appear to not have been able to handle *their* situation. The thought is barely articulated before it gives rise to another: "Why does God do this to us?" This immediately leads us to another: "Is it God who does this, or is it life?" When that question is asked, it causes one to push further than originally intended.

Once you begin to challenge even the simplest belief, it opens the door to reexamining some of the more basic beliefs you may have held dear for decades. Thinking theologically forces you out of the comfort of your living room and thrusts you into the streets – sometimes into the wilderness. It is not for the faint of heart. Yet, no discovery of any value was made by anyone who feared to leave the safety and comforts of home.

Jesus said that if we continued in his way – and did not look back (Luke 9:62) - we will learn the truth, and that truth will set us free. (John 8:32) For those willing to think theologically – honestly and earnestly, I believe that freedom draws us into a fuller relationship with the living God. Ultimate answers and understanding do not reside on the surface. They require deep digging to be revealed. It requires one to utilize John Wesley's quadrilateral (Scripture, Tradition, Experience and Reason) for whatever issue is being pursued.

1. Is the idea consistent with Scripture? This should not be confused with finding a single or small group of passages, but does it ring true with the great ideas, principles and broad themes that run through the pages. Most importantly, does it appear consistent with the teachings and person of Jesus Christ?

2. Does the idea appear to be consistent with the great teachings of the Church and the prevailing view of our world? Here, I advise caution because I believe some of these teachings went astray from those of Christ. I employ the term "Tradition" to include all of the

understandings that have been gleaned by scholars through the years. This necessarily includes science. The development of quantum physics revolutionized our understanding of this magnificent Creation of which we are a miniscule part. The first century Christians resided in a tiny world in which the Earth was the center, the Sun rotated around us and the stars were essentially like our ceiling. There was no concern for what lay outside of our little world. Space was space and time was time. They were fixed and dependable. We always define our experiences in terms of the familiar, the known. As the *known* changes, our understandings must change, as well.

3. Does the idea coincide with your own personal experience? One of the great understandings given to me at seminary was by a professor who said this: "Remember when you read the great theologians past and present, *they never are giving an objective statement about the nature of God. Rather they are sharing their own rich experience of God.*" This freed me to think for myself and to (as Paul wrote in Philippians 2:12) work out my own salvation in fear and trembling. If one accepts Jesus as in some way especially ordained to speak on God's behalf, then he – and only he – can be accepted as authoritative. Even then one must remember that all statements attributed to him are second hand at best. Questions I learned to ask while learning to be an historian were these: What was the writer's purpose in writing what he did? How do we know that he is accurate – that we can trust his words to be true? There are methods for arriving at reasonably accurate conclusions to these and others. I encourage the reader to do so in so far as possible – with my writing as well as those I shall cite.

4. Does the idea make any sense? This is why I include all disciplines of learning. The world has changed enormously since Wesley's day. Science was in its infancy and had not yet displaced the teachings of the Judaic/Christian religions as the dominant paradigm. Wesley, himself, thought outside of the box built by Calvinism. The prevailing theology held the doctrine of Predestination. This claimed that

> every soul – every person – was predestined at birth either to end up in heaven or in hell. One had no control over his or her ultimate fate. Wesley's common sense told him this was not true. Either humanity had some ability to control its own fate, or life, as Shakespeare said, "is a tale told by an idiot: full of sound and fury, signifying nothing." So ask yourself if the idea being offered makes any sense. Does it fit into your picture of reality and your understanding of God *as revealed by Jesus Christ?*

Every one of us starts the spiritual journey in a different place. No two paths can be identical. The Hindu faith understands that and allows for that. It offers a variety of Yogas from which to choose.[6] Hinduism offers Karma Yoga for the physically active (the discipline of Work}; Bhakti Yoga for the emotionally centered {the discipline of Love}; Raja Yoga for the mentally disciplined {the discipline of self-restraint } and Jnana Yoga for the mystic or spiritually sensitive (the discipline of experiential knowledge). It is well past the time when we who call ourselves Christians should recognize that fact, as well. We have differing gifts – differing ways of growing and learning. Jesus never told people they must join a group or believe certain things. He told and showed them how to live in a manner that would draw them into spiritual unity with God our Father, and he extended the invitation for *everyone* to do so. He called this state of unity with God "The Kingdom of God." Each of us must necessarily find and carve out our own path. In doing so, we will develop different ways to express our understanding. We will also have varied interpretations of the experience of God. That is expected and acceptable. No two children coming from the same family will have identical understandings of their parents or even their shared experiences. There should, however, be agreement on the essentials.

Some pilgrims seem to follow a rather direct path. Their journey begins in early childhood and then moves steadily in an upward direction. There is no sudden realization of "being saved," any more than they have a memory of having suddenly realized they loved their parents. To them, it seems to have always been that way. Many of us lived out the role of the Prodigal. We

6 Yoga means a yoke or discipline.

abandoned the faith, probably in our teens or early adulthood. Then there was a moment of "turning back home." We may have a deeper awareness of the special moment, and even be more aware of the importance of our faith. However, our faith is not necessarily any more real – any more significant – because of that. There also are those who do not encounter Christ until later in life. Their path and their story will be different, but the reality of their faith needs be no more nor less significant than that of those who followed a different path.

So why should we learn to think theologically? Because when we think about life in its long view, its purpose and worthy values, it shapes our growth. It determines what kind of person we will become in this life and the next. I am convinced that far too many sincere people waste their time upon this earth. They have been led to believe that Heaven is their ultimate goal and that simply believing properly and behaving themselves for the brief time they reside here, they can obtain it. Far too many well-intentioned people blend the Christian teachings with their personal and political values to form a comfortable philosophy of life. They may become a bit more charitable, but in far too many cases are not distinguishable from their secular/pagan neighbors. There is no spiritual growth, no actual drawing nearer to God. Eternity will come as a shock to them. Thinking theologically is the beginning of actually focusing one's life to become a genuine disciple of the Man of Galilee we call the Christ. Only the actual living of that life, however, produces fruit.

So, again, I invite you to think with me as together we explore what it means to be a follower of Jesus in today's world.

Section One

THE EARLY YEARS

First, I want to make this point clear: I am not attempting to dissuade anyone from a faith or expression of faith with which they feel comfortable. If they believe their faith moves them toward a closer relationship with the God of Jesus Christ, *and in the course of doing that causes them to* become more Christ-like I celebrate the faith they claim. What I am offering is for those who believe the faith of their childhood does not address the realities of their lives, or in some way falls short of their needs. There are legitimate alternative ways of interpreting Scripture and understanding many of our doctrines or beliefs. I propose that many of these doctrines are outdated and meaningless, and that some are a hindrance to our spiritual growth. I hope to free the reader and offer tools for working out your own salvation, perhaps with less fear and trembling than Paul implied. At the conclusion of some chapters I will offer a summary of what I hoped I conveyed. At the end of others I will suggest points to ponder and perhaps discuss.

A brief history of how the early church organized itself seems to me to be a good place to begin this journey. Until we understand how we got here, we cannot begin to find a way forward. Most of us tend to think of our present understandings and practices as "having always been." This definitely is not true. It is not true in our history as a nation. It is not true in respect to our present state of religious faith and practice. The United States is a very different country today because it was primarily settled by Western Europeans in the 16th and 17th centuries, than if it been settled by the people of some other area or some other time. The same can be said for our form of Christianity. As the culture changes, so do the understandings, values, habits and expectations of the people.

I recall a young, Korean seminary student relating his experience of speaking to an American congregation. His text was, "Be still and know that I am God." He decided to use a well-known American axiom as a means for setting his message in a familiar and acceptable American concept. At the conclusion of his sermon some of the congregation, in the process of thanking him, mentioned that they had never thought of it that way before. When he pursued this thought he realized his interpretation of the American axiom was exactly opposite of theirs. The axiom? "A rolling stone gathers no moss." We Americans, of course, take that as a reason to remain busy. He, however, took it as a means to "Be still and know that I am God." Moss, for him, represented maturity and character. A culture's worldview, values, and customs are quite determinative in deciding how a message will be shaped.

This is just a brief example of the effect of culture upon our understandings, values and habits. Now I will offer a way in which a culture's theology is changed by the circumstances of life and individuals reactions to these:

In the aftermath of the Civil War, Christian optimism was high. The last half of the 20th century was one of great zeal. Christians believed they were on the verge of ushering in the Kingdom of God. The hymn writers of that era were positive and enthusiastic about the role of the Church. "Rescue the perishing, care for the dying" rang from the church pews. Christians were the Body of Christ, doing his work around the world. A new form of the faith that one might call *optimistic liberalism* appeared. Then along came the First World War. Optimism about humanity's goodness faded quickly. Young theologians like Carl Barth, abandoned liberalism and began believing and professing that humanity was totally depraved and could do nothing apart from God's grace. In America, a young preacher-theologian named Norman Vincent Peale had a totally different perspective on life and wrote his best seller, *The Power of Positive Thinking*. Essentially, he was the corrective for the negativism that was gripping American Christianity. Years later, while Barth's Neo-Orthodoxy was still a powerful influence in American Protestantism, another young, optimistic preacher-theologian named Robert Schuller, picked up Peale's mantle and began to share that message of optimism in California. He called his television program *The Hour of Power,* and proclaimed that humanity had more power than most people imagined. In that time and place, the message resonated with enough people to make his movement quite successful. Unfortunately, in today's world we have self-proclaimed theologians whose offerings seem to be shaped by the desire to please people by justifying personal values that have no real Scriptural basis. For me, this smacks of the warning to be aware of false prophets (Matthew 7:15, 1 John 4:1-6, 2 Peter 2:1-3).

What I am trying to share is my understanding that Christian theology is not static. It is not a single set of teachings that was decided upon by some wise council more than a thousand years ago, anymore than science is static and must abide by the Laws developed by Isaac Newton in the 18th century. Christian theology is dynamic! It takes the stuff of the Gospel writings and molds it into something that is worthy, relevant and empowering *for its present time and place.*

All that said, I will bypass some of the details that were involved in the development of each branch of early Christianity. Hopefully I will present enough to give you the main influences as they affect today's reality. For a variety of reasons the early church quickly broke into differing segments. Different cultures perceive and interpret the identical event in very different ways. As with my young Korean friend, the values of one culture are not necessarily the values of another. Some values, such as those in the Ten Commandments and The Golden Rule are universal. Others are not, and might even be inappropriate when transferred to another culture. Religions do not reshape an entire culture; they tend to interact, shaping and being shaped at the same time. When the Jewish-rooted faith of Jesus was introduced into a Hellenistic world it was akin to taking a computer program designed for Windows and making it work on an iMac. It required rewriting, and when rewritten it did not operate in the same manner.

The underlying message of this section that I do not want you to miss is this: *Christianity began as a dynamic movement focused upon the life, teachings, death and resurrection of a single man.* The earliest Gospel account, Mark, offers no clear explanation of its meaning. This was to be worked out by those who realized the power of this experience and wished to incorporate it for themselves. When Paul wrote his experience of the Risen Christ, he was careful to speak as a Jew to the Jews, and to those not under the Law as one not under the Law (1 Corinthians 9:19-22). Those not under Jewish Law would not understand the work of Jesus as those who were. Working out the relevant meaning and implications of Jesus' earthly life is the task of every generation in every culture.

Much of the confusion and failure of today's churches is caused by those who wish to retreat to a past era instead of fashioning a faith for today.

Chapter One

The Jerusalem Church

The Jerusalem Church is fairly well described in the Book of Acts. However, some facts are not stated clearly, so the casual reader may misunderstand what was happening there. A first, obvious fact is that the leader of that church was James, the brother of Jesus. Peter and John are portrayed as the leaders, and perhaps they were in the very early days. However, James makes an appearance in Chapter 15. Paul and Barnabas went to Jerusalem to make a case that the non-circumcised can be saved as followers of Jesus. In a court-like setting Peter presents a case for them, citing his experience with Cornelius. Paul and Barnabas then made their presentation. At their conclusion, James rose and pronounced his judgment. This appears to have settled the matter. Peter presented his testimony, but it is James who passed judgment. From that moment on it is evident to the careful reader that it was James the brother of Jesus, not Peter, who governed that congregation. In his letter to the Galatians, Paul wrote that "when Cephas[1] came to Antioch, I opposed him face to face, because he was clearly in the wrong. For until certain persons came from James he was taking his meals with the gentile Christians; but when they came he began to hold back and became aloof; because he was afraid of the advocates of circumcision." (Galatians 2:11-12) Peter appeared to have been a powerful spokesperson for the faith. It was he who addressed the

1 *Cephas* was the Hebrew name for Rock. *Peter* (Greek *Petros*) also meant *Rock,* the name Jesus gave Simon.

crowds at Pentecost and at later times.[2] However, he obviously was not the person in charge of the Jerusalem congregation of Christians or he would not have backed away from his practice of dining with Gentiles when James' representatives arrived on the scene. James' nickname was "James the Just" because he had the reputation of adhering to the letter of the Law. In contrast, the Book of Acts relates how Simon Peter traveled to visit a Roman centurion named Cornelius and baptized this uncircumcised Gentile. Had Peter been the actual head of the Jerusalem church the remainder of the Book of Acts might have been written differently. We do not know when James arrived in Jerusalem, or how he became the leader of the early Christians. There is much speculation but absolutely no evidence. The passage that proclaims Simon Peter would be the head of the Christian Church is found in Matthew 16:13-20. The parallel passage from Mark 8:27-30 has no mention of Peter adding "The Son of the Living God" or any of the words designating Simon Peter to be the head of the Church. Since the gospel of Mark is recognized to be the memoirs of Simon Peter, one might think Peter would have mentioned it had it actually occurred. The Gospel of Matthew was written at least forty years after the Resurrection by someone who obviously had not traveled with Jesus.[3]

At this point I want to introduce you to a term you will encounter often in these writings: Hellenism. Technically the Hellenistic period was the classical Greek era that ran from Alexander's death (323 B.C.) until the rise of Rome circa 146 B.C. As a practical matter its influence ran into the 4th and 5th centuries A.D. The philosophical foundations which defined the world were Platonic and Stoic, both Greek philosophies. The universal language also was Greek. By the 2nd and 3rd centuries the Roman culture had blended in to change the mores and values. Still, historians tend to use the terms Hellenistic or Hellenism to describe the intellectual culture of that era. We have no similar word to describe our American culture. If we did it might be *Anglo-American.* The dominant European influence on our culture is English. Its language is the primary language of the population, as Greek was for the Romans. Its form of law gave shape to theirs. English culture gave the basic shape to our culture. Not French,

---

2 Acts 3: 11-26

3 See Chapter 7 on Scripture

Spanish, Italian or German, even though the people of these nations helped to settle American soil. It is in this sense that historians properly use the term Hellenist to describe the Roman culture at that time.

The rationale for selecting Hellenist deacons does not stand up under careful scrutiny. Acts 6:1 states, "During this period when disciples were growing in number, there was a disagreement between those of them that spoke Greek and those who spoke the language of the Jews." Luke was not present at that time. What he knows is what he has been told by others. He explains: "The former complained that their widows were being overlooked in the daily distribution." (Acts 6:1). He then explains that the Twelve decided to appoint seven deacons (servants) to perform the task of caring for those women. However, the first recorded act of one of those deacons, Stephen, was to speak against the Jewish traditions, for which he was stoned to death (Acts 6:8-7:60). Then in Chapter 8 we read of these deacons being chased from Jerusalem and Philip preaching in Samaria with "Great Power." It should be apparent to any thoughtful reader that the disagreement mentioned by Luke was not one of food distribution but of theological interpretation. The Hellenistic mind was not wired to understand and accept the Jewish interpretation of the meaning of Jesus' life, death and resurrection. Thus began the first of an endless stream of church schisms.

When Jerusalem fell to the Romans in 70 A.D., Antioch became the center of the Jewish element of Christianity. The Hellenists moved into Europe and quickly found their Eastern and Western areas separated by philosophy and culture.

Summary

The original Jewish/Christian community in Jerusalem was short-lived. The faith quickly spread to other cultures, and from that base eventually became a world religion. The Hellenistic interpretations dominated Christianity from that time forward, even with their many subdivisions.

Chapter Two

Antiochian Christianity

With the collapse of Jerusalem, Antioch became the heir to the original faith of the Jerusalem Christians. The city was a favorite of the Roman emperors, who thought of it as a "second Rome." It was an attractive city in many ways: metropolitan and prosperous, it attracted the young and ambitious. However, like most large, prosperous cities, it had its ghettos, its pockets of poverty and despair. It was here, among the poor and the outcasts where Christianity settled and began to grow. These early followers of Jesus cared for the downtrodden, the lost and lonely. They took seriously Jesus' call to compassion for all and practiced it as a basic attribute of their faithfulness, following the simple teachings of Jesus and his first followers. As a result, early Christianity served to stabilize the large cities of the Roman Empire by instilling a new ethic into their culture. The Christians introduced charity, caring community and hope. Their faith was simple and pragmatic. They were not interested in the mystical dimensions of the faith. As with the fundamentals of Judaism, they were more interested in the social moral/ethical aspects.

The Jewish Christians understood that when Jesus was referring to himself as The Son of Man he was calling himself the Second Adam.[4] In Ezekiel and the 8th Psalm, the term "Son of Man" merely emphasizes the humanity of the writer. Incidentally, the term we translate as *Man* does not suggest male gender. The Greek term is *anthropou,* which quite literally means *humanity.*

4 The original meaning of the word *Adam* denoted *humanity.*

In most instances when you read the generic term *man* in Scripture, a better translation would be *humanity*. In Daniel – a much later writing – it is obvious that "Son of Man" had attained another understanding. A tradition had developed that when God created humanity (Adam) he had made a second – "just in case." The first Adam disobeyed God and released evil on the land. The second Adam would undo that wrong and be obedient "even to the death." The followers of Jesus believed if they emulated his obedience they, too, would be raised from the dead into eternal life. It was a simple, but powerful faith.

The Didache, an early document purportedly presented the teachings of The Twelve. The Last Supper was not explained as a sacrifice, but was a simple "giving of thanks" (Greek: *Eucharisto*). There was no thought of the elements of bread and wine actually being the body and blood of Jesus Christ. This interpretation rose from the writings of a first century bishop, Ignatius of Antioch, who used the term, *medicine of our immortality*. This was picked up later by the Greek theologians to resolve some of their complex theological issues. However, the Christians in Antioch were not influenced by what would happen in the Hellenistic churches. For them, Jesus of Nazareth was The Second Adam, a fully human man who was obedient to God and personified the best qualities of humanity. This was completely consistent with the Jesus in the Gospel of Mark, incidentally.

During this period there were no written gospel accounts. We have strong evidence that the Gospel of Mark, written circa 70 A.D. was the memoirs of Simon Peter as recorded by his nephew, Mark. That gospel gave no doctrine of salvation and offered no accounts of resurrection appearances. These were later additions offered as the Church developed and evolved.

Unfortunately for that expression of faith, synagogue Judaism emerged from the ashes of Jerusalem. With the Temple destroyed and the Jews banned from living in their holy city faithful Jews moved into an extended exile with their holy scriptures and developed a new method for remaining faithful to their God. They closed the canon for all time at a council at Joppa in 70 A.D. There was some concern for the new religion that proclaimed the long awaited Messiah had appeared, and they did not want the writings of that heretical sect of the followers of the Nazarene infiltrating its way into their sacred writings. Most Jews preferred to remain with the faith expression they had known all their lives. Pharisees and Scribes became the teachers and formalized rabbinical Judaism became the norm. With the passage of time the Jewish element of Christianity simply faded into the dimness of history. What remained was a strong Hellenistic influence. Still, the church fathers of Antioch were particularly concerned that the human nature of Jesus not be absorbed into the divine. Thus began a Christological struggle that consumed the attention and energy of the Church for far too long.

Summary

The faith of Jerusalem moved to Antioch and Christians lived out their faith, caring for those in need. However, the Hellenistic element in the city eventually overpowered and altered the culture of the city. As it changed, the Judaic-Christian faith transmuted into a Hellenistic interpretation of the faith. In doing so, the original nature of the faith was forever changed. It blended the transcendent deity of the Hellenistic world with the accessible deity, YHWH, of the Jews.

Chapter Three

Eastern Christianity

Christianity in the East was centered in Alexandria in North Africa. The prevailing philosophy was Platonic. Plato taught that the physical world in which we live is but an imperfect representation of the real world that exists in the realm of The Idea. All that exists in our realm is informed of its nature by what was called its *Substance*, which existed in the eternal realm of the Idea. The philosophy believed anything that was created would eventually decay and cease to be. Only that which was uncreated and unchangeable was eternal. Life was understood within that framework. God also was understood within that framework. The simple faith of Jerusalem would not begin to address the issues seen by the Alexandrians. However, as I explained earlier, their theologians were up to the task. I do not mean to dismiss the efforts and accomplishments of these Greek theologians. They were brilliant men, working with the intellectual tools available to them in their time. They realized this new faith of the Jews carried great spiritual power and offered hope and a more profound moral/ethical framework. However, in its Jewish form it could not be acceptable to the Hellenistic mind. They sought to make sense of the resurrection event in the framework of their understanding of how the world operated. The Jewish understanding of humanity was simple: a body in which God-breathed spirit made a living soul. A physical resurrection was understandable and acceptable to the Jewish mind. God had only to breathe the spirit back into Jesus and Jesus could be resurrected. This was totally inconceivable, and therefore unacceptable, to the Hellenistic understanding of the composition of humanity. For the Hellenist, a human consisted of a body cloaked in flesh. This body contained a soul and a mind and was activated by a spirit. When the body died, the soul had the potential to be eternal. It did not require a physical body, as did the Jewish understanding. Paul attempted to address this in his letter to the church at Corinth when he wrote, "The body that is sown is perishable; the body that is raised is imperishable." (1 Corinthians 15:42). What was needed was an explanation that could allow the Hellenistic mind to accept the thought of a resurrection or continuation of the soul. Given the tools they had, they did an excellent job of making Christianity understandable and acceptable for their cultural needs.

There were other issues that put pressure on the Christian theologians: one was that the two major rival religions to Christianity were Mithraism and the cult of Isis. Both Mithras and Isis were full-fledged gods. Even allowing for the birth narratives in Matthew and Luke, Jesus was, at best, a demigod: half divine and half human. If someone wished to become involved in a newly forming religion, a complete, 100% deity certainly was more attractive than a half-deity. The other issue, of course, was that the Christians claimed to be monotheistic, but appeared to be worshipping Jesus as a god as well as worshipping the god Jesus referred to as "Father." Somehow the theologians had to resolve this apparent contradiction.

As mentioned earlier the Alexandrian theologians resolved all these issues by utilizing the technical tools of Platonic philosophy. They skillfully interpreted selected passages of Scripture to build their case. Since Scripture had no authoritative standing at that time, they also included the writings of the early martyrs. These writings were deemed authoritative by the fact that their writers had borne witness (were martyred) to their faith by sacrificing their lives. An early martyr, Bishop Ignatius of Antioch, had written a series of letters on his way to Rome to be executed for his Christian belief. In his letter to the Ephesians he wrote:

> . . . join me in the common meeting in grace from his name, in one faith and in Jesus Christ, "who was of the family of David according to the flesh," the Son of Man and the Son of God, so that you obey the bishop and the elders with an undisturbed mind, breaking one bread, which is the *medicine of immortality*,

> (italics mine) the antidote that we should not die, but live forever in Jesus Christ.[5] (Ignatius to the Ephesians xx)

They interpreted Ignatius' statement about "the medicine of immortality" to mean that when Jesus said, "This is my body" and "This is my blood" at the final meal in the upper room, he actually meant the underlying reality of those elements which today we might call *essence*, but then was called *substance*, actually had been *transubstantiated* to be Christ's body and blood. All that was left for these resourceful theologians to do then was to find a means for declaring Jesus to be uncreated – eternal. They found the term they needed in the Gospel of John: *Logos* (English: *Word*). This was a term found in Stoic philosophy which signified what, for the purpose of simplification, is often called "The World Soul." It is the dimension of deity that represents the will and nature of God. With amazing intellectual agility the theologians determined that the Logos incarnate (The Son) was of the same substance as the Father, and thus was Eternal! This was contrary to the bulk of Scriptural evidence, but it served their purpose, so it stuck (The printing press had not been invented. Most people were illiterate and few scriptures were available). The debate over whether The Son was of the same substance or a similar substance raged for a few hundred years. Theoretically it was resolved at the Council of Nicaea in 325 A.D. with the formulation and acceptance of the Nicene Creed.[6] As a practical matter it continues to be a subject of debate.

---

5 From this simple statement we are able to see that the original simple Christology of the Jewish remnant that perceived Jesus as the Second Adam had evolved to include his also being the Son of God. These terms are mutually exclusive. Jesus could not be both the second human created by God and God's actual Son. He either was created (a creature) or he was eternal (uncreated). We also see that the memorial Eucharist has assumed more mystical dimensions. This represents the blending of Jewish thought with Hellenism.

6 I believe in one God, the Father Almighty, maker of heaven and earth, visible and invisible, and in one Lord, Jesus Christ, the only begotten Son of God, begotten by the Father before all worlds. God of God, Light of Light, very God of very God, begotten not made, being of one substance with the Father by whom all things were made. Who for us men and our salvation came down from heaven and was incarnated by the Holy Spirit of the Virgin Mary and was made man, and was crucified also for us under Pontius Pilate. He suffered and was buried, and the third day he rose again according to the Scriptures, and ascended into heaven, and sits at the right hand of God the Father, and he shall come again with glory to judge both the quick and the dead whose kingdom shall have no end. And I believe in the Holy Spirit the Lord and Giver of Life, who proceeded from the Father and the Son, who with the Father and Son together is worshipped and glorified, who spoke by the prophets. And I believe in one holy Catholic and Apostolic Church. I acknowledge one baptism for the remission of sins, and I look forward to the resurrection of the dead, and the life of the world to come. (Spurgeon translation)

Those finely crafted, but now meaningless, explanations of the Nicene Creed are repeated in many churches every Sunday.

The Eastern Church drew much of its theology from the Gospel of Mark, who, according to tradition, founded the church in Alexandria. They therefore had no doctrine of atonement. Instead, their formula for salvation was stated simply as "The Divine became human that the human might become divine." At the moment of baptism, they believed the Holy Spirit joined with the newly baptized ones to guide and empower them to become the fullness of the image in which they were created. Guilt and confession are not a significant part of their thinking.

Summary

The Eastern Church relied heavily upon the writings of Mark, who was credited as having been the founder; therefore they had no doctrine of Jesus' death as an act of atonement. Instead, they focused upon Jesus' mission of enabling people to become Christ-like.

Chapter Four

The Western Church

The Western Church had no early center. Rome rose to prominence during the time of dispute between Antioch and Alexandria. Their bishops served as mediators, and with the passage of time the idea of looking to Rome for leadership became an accepted principle. The early leaders of the congregation in Rome, incidentally, were known as presiders or presidents rather than as bishops. If Simon Peter actually had been the founder and leader of that church he would have been a presider – not a bishop. One might also check out Paul's letter to the Romans (Chapter16). Paul fills the conclusion of his letter with specific greetings to members at Rome, *but never mentions Simon Peter*. Does it not seem strange that in this attempt to create a sense of connectedness and unity by his many personal references, he never mentions or greets the head of their congregation who is a personal friend and colleague?

The prevailing philosophy that shaped the world-view of the Western world was Stoicism, with its emphasis upon natural law. When coupled with the dominance of Roman law and Jewish understanding of Torah as Law it was inevitable that the liberating message of Jesus would eventually become embodied in a legalistic framework. Remember that a new religion must adapt itself to the culture in order to be understandable and meaningful. Terms like "Second Adam" and "The Divine became human that the human might become divine" mean absolutely nothing to the Western Hellenistic mind. Paul wrote in terms understandable to the times and culture when he wrote that he sought to be as "one under the Law to those under the Law (Jews), and to those outside the Law as one outside the law" (Gentiles) (1 Corinthians 9: 20-21). For Paul, the law was the Jewish Law as recorded in the Torah. However, in the Western Church the term quickly evolved into Papal or Canon Law. The interpretation of Jesus' death as a sacrifice of atonement developed and the communion table that once celebrated the Last Supper as The Eucharist or *Giving of Thanks*, a simple celebration of life together in Christ, became a sacrificial altar with a liturgy laden in guilt. I referred to this in an earlier chapter, but this seems the appropriate time to expand on the *Didache*.[7] Tradition claims that this book of teachings had its source with the original Twelve Apostles, as they were reconstituted after the Resurrection. To that extent it represents the earliest understanding of the basics of the Christian faith. The *Didache* states this form for celebrating the Lord's Supper:

> *And concerning the Eucharist, hold Eucharist thus: First, concerning the cup, "We give thanks to you, our Father, for the holy vine of David, thy child which you did make known to us through Jesus, your son. To you be glory forever. And concerning the broken bread: we give thanks, our Father, for the life and knowledge you made known to us through Jesus your child. To you be glory forever. As this broken bread was scattered upon the mountains, but was brought back together and became one, so let your congregation be gathered together from the ends of the earth into your kingdom, for yours is the power and the glory through Jesus Christ forever."* (my translation of the Greek)

There is not a hint of the meal being understood as a sacrifice. It is more of a memorial, as expressed in Luke 22:19 or by Paul in 1 Corinthians 11:24. No council ever declared the Atonement as an official doctrine of the Church. It simply slipped in somewhere along the way. It should also be apparent that Jesus was not thought of as divine in this ritual. Both Jesus and David were referred to as *God's child*, an ambiguous term, at best. Atonement eventually became the more dominant theory because it spoke to an inner need for

---

7 Lake, Kirsopp, trans. *The Apostolic Fathers*, Cambridge: Harvard University Church, 1912

forgiveness that most people seem to carry around inside of themselves. This thought will be more fully explored a bit later. By the end of the first century, that simple understanding was changed, and the table where the Eucharist was held as a memorial meal became an altar upon which Christ's sacrifice was reenacted. In his letter to the Smyrnaeans, Ignatius complains about a group of believers who do not share the same belief:

> They abstain from the Eucharist and prayer because they do not confess that the Eucharist is the flesh of our Savior Jesus Christ who suffered for our sins. (Ignatius to the Smyrnaeans VII)

Frankly, these dissidents appear to me to be more in tune with the original Antiochian Christians. I believe the Hellenists finally just outnumbered them and, therefore changed the culture. When that occurred, the new culture required a new expression. The memorial meal and the Second Adam faded from the scene.

The original meaning of the cross and resurrection was *Christus Victor.* Christ had triumphed over death. A mortal human had escaped from the bonds of death; consequently Death (Thanatos) no longer could imprison humans. This doctrine is embedded in one of the most famous Easter hymns, "Christ the Lord is Risen Today." The words are these: "Death in vain forbids him rise. Christ has opened Paradise." That concept had no meaning for the Hellenists, and has no meaning for later generations and had to be discarded.

Eventually, the elders of the church evolved into priests who stood between God and humanity as intermediaries. By the end of the 2nd century the North African theologian, Tertullian, declared in his letter against heresies that, "there is no salvation outside the church." The early church gathered in basilicas fashioned after the town meeting halls complete with congregational interaction. The table was in the center, and the clergy acted more as servers (deacons) to the laity. Eventually an apse that separated the clergy from the laity was added to the basilicas. The clergy were elevated to priests as a sacrificial altar replaced the table. In time, the laity were reduced to passive recipients of a church-bestowed grace. By the 11th century pews were introduced. The laity sat passively through the service, and the dominance of the priesthood was complete.

If you visit Ravenna in Italy, the ancient capital of the Western Roman Empire, the transition can be seen in the church mosaics. From the earliest mosaic in the Mausoleum of Galla Placiddia to the Basilica of Apollinare in Classe the transition of a very human appearing Jesus as a Good Shepherd intimately caring for his flock to a non-human appearing Jesus-as-judge, remote in the heavens with the Bishop Apollinare serving as the Good Shepherd guiding the sheep through the doorway of the church is clearly evident. I still vividly recall my first visit to that ancient capital city in the summer of 1970. The simple mosaic of Jesus as the Good Shepherd in the mausoleum stood in sharp contrast to the later Byzantine mosaics I saw elsewhere. Any sense of Jesus as a human being was lost. There was no trace of emotion – except sternness, perhaps. I paused, realizing that these figures were the images of Jesus that the worshippers saw every time they worshipped. There was no gentle Jesus meek and mild; no "Let the little children come unto me," Jesus who offered hospitality or comfort; no wounded Jesus carrying a cross; or smiling Jesus waving at the crowds as he rode into Jerusalem on a donkey. There was only this distant, uncaring, unseeing figure with large, unfocused eyes. I shuddered as though a sudden chill had filled the building. This man those people worshipped was not one I could love or care about. "How did we ever stray so far?" I asked myself as I continued to wander the streets of this once capital city of the Western Roman Empire.

It must be noted that throughout the checkered history of the Western Church there were individuals with outstanding character, wisdom, dedication and insight. With the assumption of great power after the fall of the Roman Empire, the church attracted those who were drawn toward power rather than service. This resulted in a period when many of the church leaders were self-indulgent and corrupt, more interested in satisfying their own needs and ambitions than in following the leadership of Jesus Christ. The Crusades, Spanish Inquisition, solicitation of Indulgences, and taxation of prostitutes were the more notable shameful activities of this era. By the time of the Reformation, the church leaders were among the wealthiest and most powerful people on earth.[8]

---

8 An example of this wealth can be seen by any visitor to Rome, or anyone who owns a computer. The Villa d'Este in Tivoli was given as a consolation prize to Cardinal Ippolito II d'Este when he failed to win the papacy circa 1550 A.D.

During that same visit to Ravenna I made an earlier stop in Cologne, Germany. There I saw my first honest-to-God cathedral. It was an overwhelming experience! I had never encountered a building so huge – so grand – in all my life. We were scheduled to depart early the next morning, but I had to see that wonderful building one more time. I rose early the next morning and found my way through the winding streets by following the magnificent tower that could be seen from anywhere, it seemed. I brought out my field glasses, found a place to sit, and gazed at the building, intently trying to understand what it was saying. Dr. Laeuchli, God bless him, had taught us to read architecture to understand its message. This magnificent edifice was proclaiming its nobility and power to all who could view it. Then the deep part of my mind asked: "How did those simple fishermen and merchants of Galilee become these nobles and warriors who adorned the walls?" "What happened along the way that mutated our faith from a simple, liberating and empowering spiritual movement . . . to . . . this . . . this total distortion of what Jesus proclaimed and for which he died?" "Foxes have their dens and birds their nests, but the Son of Man has no place – no place at all . . . to lay his head." (Luke 9:58) From a feeling of excitement to a feeling of despair – in one easy viewing. Again, it must be remembered that even in the worst of times there were many faithful followers of the Man of Galilee who cared for one another, and ministered to their congregations. Clergy and laity alike lived the message and carried the Church even when the Church was not capable of carrying itself.

The reaction to the misdeeds of the leadership erupted into the Protestant Reformation that forever changed the face and character of the Western Church. Various leaders arose, each offering their own personal understanding of the Gospel. Some were solidly grounded in an understanding of Scripture and church history. Some were not. Each attracted loyal adherents and the church began a process of fragmentation that continues to this day. Some are grounded in an understanding of the development of doctrine and scripture, and some appear to have no understanding or interest in those aspects of their faith. This has resulted in creating a range of Christianity that is so broad in its theological spectrum that the term *Christianity* must have modifiers in order to convey any understanding of what it means. Its adherents range in character from compassionate, liberating and empowering to harshly judgmental, controlling and disabling. "They will know that we are Christians by our love" is no longer a universally accepted criterion.

Points to Ponder

Since Jesus did not offer a reason for his death, how would you go about finding or developing a suitable rationale? Bear in mind that the explanation from the Jerusalem Christians made no sense to you and those of your culture. Actually, if you wish to discard the atonement explanation, that is precisely what you must do. What do you think is the reason Jesus chose to die by crucifixion rather than return to Galilee where he could have lived out his life as a healer/rabbi?

Chapter Five

Gnosticism, the Forgotten Theology

Gnosticism was one of the early branches of Christianity, and the Gospel of Thomas is one of their most significant writings. This writer believes that the so-called Gospel of Thomas had as good a claim to canonization as the writings of John. Those who have only a cursory understanding of the Patristic era of the Church call Gnosticism a heresy. The primary source for understanding Gnosticism was a second century bishop of Lyons, named Irenaeus who wrote *Against Heresies*, a work defining – and demeaning - those theologies he deemed heretical. There are many, however, who believe Gnosticism was one of a few legitimate expressions of the faith. The patristic scholars, in particular, have reason to suspect that Irenaeus' issue with the Gnostics was more than theological. The Gnostics did not recognize designated authority. Rather, they responded to what they believed was spiritual authority, following the model of Jesus, "who spoke as one with authority," (Matthew 7:29) so the Gnostics preferred this type of leader. The term gnostic suggests *knowing through experience* as opposed to *knowing about* – or from a teaching. In one of his letters to the bishop of Rome (there was no one leader of the church during this era) Irenaeus complained that the Gnostics neither informed him of their meetings nor invited him to participate. As the bishop who presided at every church worship service he felt slighted, to say the least. His examples of Gnosticism are fairly accurate, but he either was unaware of other branches or chose not to use them. As with any widespread faith, there are some far more worthy expressions than others.

Until the discovery of the Nag Hammadi Library in 1945 the only information we had about Gnosticism was from those early writers who opposed their theology. The process of translating ancient Coptic texts into understandable English and then being able to study and live with the thoughts sufficiently to critique them required decades to complete. It is understandable that so many practicing clergy today only think of Gnosticism as a forbidden heresy. However, I have found the teachings of Gnosticism to be quite compatible with the teachings of Carl Jung, the Swiss psychiatrist. In the 20th century, Carl Jung discovered the essence of Gnostic thought in the emerging science of psychology and incorporated it into his system. When I first encountered Jung's writings back in the early 1960's my reaction was that Jung offered an intellectual foundation for understanding and entering into Western spirituality. Everything I have learned about Jungian thought since that time has served to confirm that opinion. One book in my collection of Jungian writings is entitled, *The Gnostic Jung and the Seven Sermons to the Dead*. In the epilogue he cites Francis Bacon as a means of summing up the book, "Let the mind, so far as it can, be open to the fullness of the mysteries; let not the mysteries be constrained to fit the narrower confines of the mind."[9] To this he adds the thought that, for the early Gnostics *gnosis* was a knowing of the heart – not the mind. I would suggest that it reaches beyond that. It is an inner knowing which has the quality of being experiential. Jung was once asked if he believed in God. His response was, "No. I *know* God."

Gnosticism was a philosophy in the ancient world that preceded Christianity. It appealed to those with independent personalities who enjoyed intellectual complexity and abstraction. They interpreted the teachings of Jesus in symbolic and metaphorical ways, probing for their spiritual meanings. In their meditations and deliberations they searched inside themselves for the deeper understandings. They had no concern for being saved from their sins. Rather, they sought an experiential understanding that might be

---

9 Hoeller, Stephen A., The Gnostic Jung and the Seven Sermons to the Dead The Theological Publishing House, Wheaton, IL U.S.A. 1985.

described as helping to complete the image of God they believed to be within themselves. Simply put, they sought to become *whole*. Bear in mind that a new religion does not radically redefine a culture. It is incorporated into that culture's structure. Gnosticism incorporated the elements of Christianity into its philosophy. In that way it really was no different than what both the Eastern and Western world had done with the simple faith of the Jewish Christians who had walked with Jesus of Nazareth. It had the same right to live alongside the other expressions. However, because it was not located geographically, but dwelt in the midst of the other, larger and more established expressions of the faith, like most minority groups it was discounted, denied equal rights and branded as a heresy.

There are two basic ways in which the human mind functions. The most common is in the *linear, literal* way, dealing with concrete, straightforward practical understandings and applications. The other, less common, is intuitive which is more holistic in scope. That mind likes complexity and abstraction, dealing easily in the realm of ideas. Research revealed that approximately three quarters of the population operates in the linear, literal mode, so it was inevitable that the Church, particularly the Western Church, developed along the lines of biblical literalism. The independent, intuitive Gnostics posed a threat to the theology and hierarchy of the developing "Orthodoxy" and therefore were declared to be heretical. The Eastern mind, however, tended to be more attuned to abstract, intuitive thought, and some aspects of Gnosticism remained. In the West, many closet Gnostics found refuge in the monastic movement. Some of the more influential thinkers were nuns such as Julian of Norwich and Teresa of Avila.

The Gospel of John has many Gnostic overtones. I have already mentioned the introduction which correctly translates as "*The light came into the world but the darkness was unable to grasp it.*" Most of the spiritual implications tend to escape the understanding of the literally inclined. One of the most glaring is the gross oversimplification of the statement found in chapter 14:6: "No one comes to the Father except through me." The linear, literal reader interprets this to mean that only through the historic person of Jesus of Nazareth can one be received by God. *The introduction clearly states that John assumes this historic Jesus actually is the divine Logos cloaked in flesh.* To that end, John has Jesus saying what bad translation states as either "I am he" or "I am the one" but actually is saying "I AM."[10] Those who read John in the original Greek would understand John's view caused Jesus to be proclaiming himself to be divine. The divine Logos represents the dimension of deity that expresses the will and nature of God. Therefore when Jesus says that no one comes to the Father except through him he is stating a truism: no one spiritually moves nearer to God unless he is following the way that represents the will and nature of God. Jesus does not say one must speak his words or sing his praises, he merely states the obvious: become the same person you see in me and you will be on a spiritual path that unites you with God. Earlier John states the rule even more clearly. In John 8:32 Jesus says, "If you continue in my way you shall come to know (*gnosis*)[11] the truth and the truth shall set you free."

In his book, *The Quest for the Historic Jesus*,[12] after a monumental struggle to work through the contradictions and additions found in the Gospels, Albert Schweitzer admits the impossibility of the task. It is the distinction between knowing *about* and actually knowing because you have experienced it. The difference is profound. His final paragraph acknowledges that the historic Man of Galilee can never be fully understood by the mind alone, and points the reader to the Presence of the Risen Christ. Shortly after this, he left his chair at the university in Germany and began to serve Christ experientially as a physician in Africa.

Today's Christian Gnostic must do the inner work to understand the soul, and then the outer work to understand the Man of Galilee we call Jesus.

Conclusion

Jesus' life, death and resurrection was an exciting event. It was a potentially very powerful new and genuine tale of mythological proportions that could invigorate and offer hope to many. Those who recognized this new faith struggled to find an expression of the message that would be acceptable, understandable

---

10 I AM is the commonly accepted translation of YHWH or Yahweh.

11 *gnosis* denotes experiential understanding.

12 Schweitzer, Albert, *The Quest for the Historic Jesus*, trans. W. Montgomery, Mineola: Dover Publications, 2005

and relevant to their culture. These early theologians were talented, dedicated men. Each group succeeded in formulating doctrines that served the purpose of making this new spiritual dynamic understandable and relevant *for their time and their needs.* For many who would be followers of Jesus today, these historic teachings no longer have meaning or relevance. Over the past few decades there have been those spiritual pioneers who have been creating a new way of interpreting the story of Jesus. I shall list a few in the Bibliography.

Chapter Six

Heresies – Good and Bad

The term *heresy* is from the Greek *haeresis* which originally mean *choice* or *thing chosen.* A *heretic* was someone who either had made or was making a choice. In early Greek culture wise and secure parents encouraged their children to study the various philosophies and choose the one that best suited their understanding of themselves and their life goals. A youth might decide to follow the teachings of Plato or Socrates or to become a Stoic or a member of some other philosophic school. It would be akin to those parents today who intentionally expose their children to a variety of religions when they are in their late teens, and encourage them to make their own choice rather than living an inherited religion. Over a period of time, the term began to denote someone whose choice was different from the norm. It had no pejorative connotation. It implied an independent thinker. Irenaeus of Lyons was the first writer to use the term in a demeaning way.

At one level I encourage heretical (independent) thinking. I believe, however, that most people raised within a single religion are so conditioned that even considering changing to another expression of faith is unthinkable to them. Their understanding of the world has been thoroughly grounded in the doctrines of their faith. Change would be difficult indeed. For those who feel dissatisfied or unfulfilled by their inherited faith, however, the desire to find some better way may demand at least an exploration of other paths. In those instances I believe a bit of heresy is healthy – even therapeutic. Frankly, this book was written for healthy heretics seeking a better way.

Unhealthy heresies are the concern of this chapter. They do not necessarily represent a minority view. Rather, too often they reflect the thinking of many sincere Christians. I believe the Church's early concerns for unity led them down the wrong path. Their focus upon the nature of Jesus of Nazareth caused them to spend their time and energy debating such matters as the Nicene Controversy, *i.e.* whether Jesus' nature was similar to God's or identical to God's. The entire issue arose from a false premise: "Anything created could decay and die. Only that which was uncreated could be eternal." With that premise, the only way that it was possible for Jesus Christ to be the means for gaining eternal life was for him to have been uncreated. Since it was acknowledged that he had been born of a woman, it required some interesting intellectual gymnastics to demonstrate that his essential nature was uncreated. The words "begotten not made" state that in the creed of Nicaea, but the theology underlying that statement is anything but clear. It rests on a paradigm that no longer has any basis for existence. For two years I sat in classes discussing this. Time and time again my mind seemed to grasp what was being said, only to lose the understanding because the premise was so totally different than our current understanding of how the world operates. Sometime in my second year of doctoral studies I finally was able to hold the idea in place. Consequently, when I hear those asserting the Nicene Creed should be the required creed of our faith I really wonder if they have any idea what those words mean, e.g. "God of God, Light of Light, very God of very God, begotten not made, being of one substance with the Father." From the time of its approval at the Nicene Council in 325 A.D. heresy dealt with the varied interpretations that arose from it.

Had those early theologians paid more attention to scriptural exegeses, analyzing them, they might have decided to reexamine their premise rather than ignoring the scriptural witnesses. Those witnesses make it quite clear that Jesus is not to be confused with God. In the Garden of Gethsemane Jesus says, "Nevertheless, not my will but thine." (Luke 22:42) He makes it clear that they are separate in their wills and he believes himself to be lesser. In John 14:28, Jesus says, "The Father is greater than I." If we accept this then we are faced with a dilemma: either we have more than one God, or Jesus is not a god. We cannot have it both ways. I have read many contrived explanations, but I stay with Ockham's Razor, that the simplest explanation is the most acceptable.

Today, that 4th century premise is reversed. We now operate on the assumption that change is essential to life. Unless someone – or something - is able to adapt, modify and renew, that someone or something will decay and cease to be. The term *substance* no longer has meaning since the Platonic understanding of existence was replaced by Newton's. We do not believe there are universal substances that mystically inform matter of its nature. Today we would use the term *essence*, which we realize is non-substantive – intangible. Many a bad decision has been made based upon a false premise. Many of the misunderstandings of the Christian faith have been based upon assumptions that simply no longer have meaning under logical scrutiny.

Actually, the argument over Jesus' nature is irrelevant to the Christian faith. It is obvious that Mark perceived Jesus as a spirit-filled human; John saw him as the divine Logos of God, while Mathew and Luke viewed him as a demigod, half deity and half human. If one's Christology is critical, which one should we call a true Christian while branding the others as heretics? In focusing on this nonessential, the church lost sight of the true issues of our faith which do have a bearing on the development of our souls.

In spite of overwhelming evidence, three great heresies of the church still exist today. They are cloaked in a garb of piety and orthodoxy, but they are false – and they are destructive to the human spirit. The first is this: the religion *of* Jesus became the religion *about* Jesus. Rather than being seen as the model for humanity, Jesus is viewed by most Christians as divine and the rightful recipient of our worship. This fact, in itself, has radically altered the thrust of the early Christian church to such an extent it would not be recognized by those early Christians who followed Peter, Paul, James and John.

The second heresy is a natural outgrowth of the first. It, too, completely distorts the life-renewing message of Jesus. Its present form is the Gospel of Prosperity. It stems from the books of the Old Testament that were edited by the Deuteronomic Historian. He had a simple formula he utilized throughout his writings: those who worshipped and obeyed the God YHWH prospered and lived long, healthy lives. Those who disobeyed YHWH and/or worshipped false deities were punished in this lifetime. People believed that even in the face of overwhelming evidence to the contrary, simply because they chose to believe it – they wanted to believe it. It was both the prize and security they sought. Finally the books of Ecclesiastes and Job proclaimed that life simply did not work that way. In colonial America, Calvinism evolved into the Puritan Ethic, which, in turn, became the Spirit of Capitalism, which eventually evolved into the American Dream.

Although the religious significance has long been lost, it did have its roots in Calvin's doctrine of Predestination.[13] The idea developed that those predestined for heaven probably would be given special treatment while on earth. The earnest Calvinists tried to prosper by diligence and thriftiness to prove to themselves that they were among the elect.

These qualities tended to create prosperity, but over a period of time, the good life on earth began to outweigh the future benefits of heaven and the Puritan ethic dropped its theology and became the American Dream wherein we believe that hard work and careful use of finances can make a person wealthy. Later, the likes of Andrew Carnegie picked up the religious theme again. He traveled the country preaching his message of "The Ten Talented Man." It was his theory that the exceptionally talented person had the right to excessive wealth, even at the cost to his one talented laborers. Carnegie justified his wealth by donating money for libraries, concert halls, and other fine arts. Incidentally, he hired the Pinkerton detectives to keep his workers in line. Many fine people were severely hurt and a few slain during some of their confrontations. The very wealthy, however, thought Carnegie's message was good theology. If one thinks this through logically it actually reduces the God of Jesus Christ to some divine ATM. If one performs properly then God *must* reward the faithful for their actions. If this formula is valid, then we humans can actually control God's actions by *our* actions. Otherwise the formula does not work. God *may* – not *will* – reward the faithful. It becomes a matter of pure chance. I have known far too many pious church members who genuinely believed they could get God to answer their prayers and give them special favors because of their piety. As erroneous as it is, this is the theological foundation for today's Prosperity Theology. It is attractive because it satisfies the yearning of our own egocentricity that demands we be special.

---

13 This is not the same as Predetermination. Rather, it simply proclaims that a person is predestined for either heaven or hell at birth, and there is nothing that can be done to change that.

At every church I have served I have had question after question about what Rabbi Harold Kushner wrote *When Bad Things Happen to Good People.* As long as people insist upon shaping God as a celestial Santa Claus or ATM, that question will persist. Until we allow God to be God – far beyond our understanding - we will continue to ask the unanswerable question, like Job crying out from the ashes (Job 2:8). The only promises I recall from Scripture was that God would be with us in every experience of life, sharing, comforting, empowering and guiding us along the way. Aside from that, I recall Jesus offering us a cross – and a promise that he, too, would be with us on our journey.

In the course of this last heresy in its various forms, the spiritual message of Jesus was distorted, perverted and lost. The primary thrust of the faith proclaimed by Jesus was, "The Kingdom of God is at hand. Repent and believe this good news." The final section of this book will focus entirely upon what that simple, overused term, repent, actually means for us. For the moment, however, suffice it to say that the great spiritual struggle of this life is between the egocentricity of our conscious self and the theocentricity of our unconscious self. [14]

The third heresy is the most divisive and debilitating of the heresies. It is the unspoken belief that any one of us can possibly comprehend and precisely define infinite God. Yet we quickly and strongly deny that other expressions of faith are valid. In large families the children may call their parents by different names. Some might say "mother" or "father;" others may say, "mom and dad" or "mommy and daddy." My own three daughters had an opportunity for a "Just Sisters" getaway some time after they had grown and had families of their own. One daughter returned and said, "It was the elephant and the three blind men all over again." You may recall the story about the three blind men who each grasped a different part of the elephant and then shared his experience with the other two. One claimed the animal was like a wall, another said it was like a tree trunk while the third compared it with a snake. They argued and argued and finally parted in anger. Had they carefully listened and respected the others' experience they would have gained

14 Theocentricity is the term I coined to define the divine love of God. I believe it is of our true selves. The conscious self is egocentric. Our inner Image of God is theocentric.

a better idea of the nature of the elephant. So it was with my daughters, except they did listen and gained a better understanding of who their parents actually were. When I taught World Religions at Henry Ford Community College in Dearborn Michigan, I often was reminded of that tale. Now, when I participate in San Antonio's annual Martin Luther King, Jr. interfaith worship I think of it again. Christian Protestants and Catholics, Hindus, Jews, Muslims, Buddhists, Sikhs, Baha'is and some other religions and sects gather together to share common values and dreams and to celebrate a life they believed personified their beliefs. I cannot help but believe that if we listened to one another instead of ignoring and demeaning one another our understanding of God would grow and grow until finally we could conceive of a God large enough to embrace all humanity – all creatures large and small.

It is that old bugaboo egocentricity that is at the root of this heresy as it is at the root of every sin – every shortfall of our spiritual growth.

Points to Ponder

The theology of the Church is not a static entity. What works in one culture does not necessarily work in another. The forced exclusion of minority faiths or expressions of a faith is dictatorship. In the fourth century, Bishop Athanasius, often considered the great defender of Christian Orthodoxy, demanded that those who would be faithful followers of the church destroy all copies of those texts he deemed heretical. Fortunately, at least one priest ignored this and buried the texts in what now is known as the Nag Hammadi Library. Without these texts scholars would be at the complete mercy of those earlier writers who wrote from their limited experiences and personal agendas.

The independent thinker was admired in older societies that felt secure in their beliefs. It is the independent thinker who is capable of thinking outside the established box to offer new ideas and new perspectives. Jesus obviously was an independent thinker. Galileo was an independent thinker. Our own history extolls the Declaration of Independence. Our Bill of Rights demands freedom of press and speech, encouraging freedom of thought in order to keep us from becoming enslaved. It was Hitler and Stalin who burned and banned the books. Unfortunately, there were times in our history that the Christian Church did the same thing. Even today there are people who will not read a book because someone perceived as authority told them it was heretical.

> *If you continue in my way then you are my disciples indeed, and*
> *You shall come to know the truth and the truth shall set you free.*
> (John 8:32)

Chapter Seven

Scripture

Too much of our traditional faith is predicated on the assumption that all tales found in both the Old and New Testament are literally and historically true. This creates a false understanding and expectation of the manner in which God operates in our world. As these expectations are not met, God seems less and less dependable and meaningful to our lives. Today's average Christian has little or no understanding of how our Holy Scriptures came into being. Far too many believe the false myths they were taught as children, because they never questioned their truth or attempted to understand why they existed. The Western mind is prone to thinking, writing and teaching in a straightforward, literal style. We deal with facts. The Eastern mind, which includes the Hebrews of biblical days, prefers to teach wisdom rather than facts. Wisdom, they believe, gives the students a basis for utilizing and analyzing facts. Wisdom helps one to live well. Wisdom is not dispensed in the same manner as facts. Wisdom is conveyed through tales in which the listeners learn for themselves the lessons being passed along. Wisdom stories are never to be understood literally, anymore than the parables of Jesus were to be taken literally. During one of my trips to Israel a tour guide pointed out the inn of the Good Samaritan to our group. I was the tour leader and did not want such garbage being taught as truth. Incredulous, I asked him if he really believed that. He stiffened and replied, "Absolutely!" I turned to the group and pointed down the road: "There is where the Levite crossed to the other side," I announced. Needless to say, that guide and I did not develop a warm relationship. The inn, incidentally, appeared to have been constructed in the 1800's.

Much of what passes as accepted Christian teachings and beliefs have no biblical basis, but were pious wishes that eventually became accepted truths. The most flagrant of these is the so-called Rapture. This was the brainchild of John Nelson Darby, a Plymouth Brethren clergyman in the 1830's. John had no particular training as a theologian. His teaching appeals to people who like to think of themselves as special. Also, during difficult times there always are a group of people who would love to be rescued. Many failures of traditional Christianity have been generated by these non-biblical misunderstandings. If one digs into them they see that their foundation is a need to feel special and/or secure.

Jewish Scriptures

These developed over a period of centuries. The *Torah*, or so-called "Books of Moses" are the first five books of the Old Testament. They were primarily derived from four major sources. German scholars, using the tools of modern literary scholarship recognized four distinct writing styles within the original manuscripts. Anyone who reads contemporary authors easily understands this. They recognize the unique styles of their favorite authors immediately. The German scholars called them Jahwist (J), Elohist (E), Deuteronomist source (D), and Priestly source (P). The basic theory is that the E and J writers were gathered together and edited by the D writers into a single collection. They also used oral traditions and bits and pieces of tales and traditions they gleaned along the way. Later, these were organized, added to and edited by the P writers. Over time, these five collections of writings became known as the *Torah* or *Law*.

The Jahwist writer was from Judah and the name used for God was JHVH (YHWH in English). His writings are dated circa 950 B.C.E. He wrote the second Creation story (Genesis 2-11), which is obviously far more primitive than Genesis 1 that was written by the Priestly authors (circa 600-400 B.C.E). In that story, God fashions Adam from clay and then creates a life-sized Eve from Adam's rib. He sets them in a garden, but when they disobey Him God casts them unto the earth as punishment. In the later tale, God creates humanity, and grants them dominion over the earth. The Jahwist source wrote the Abraham stories that present his heirs as chosen to be protected and to become a great nation. He emphasizes the flow of sin and its consequences and grace in human history.

The Elohist writer was from Israel (also known as Ephraim) and his name for God was Elohim. His writings are dated circa 850 B.C.E. His primary themes are fourfold: 1. Fear of God. 2. Prophetic leadership. 3. Covenant. 4. A theology of history focused upon Israel.

The Deuteronomist source wrote circa 550 B.C.E. Those writers draw from earlier sources and appear to be connected to the source of the law found in the Temple during the reign of Josiah, 649-609 B.C.E. Deuteronomy literally means the second giving of the law. The writers of this created what is often termed the Deuteronomic Theory of History. This overly simplified view proclaimed that those who are obedient to God will prosper, while those who are disobedient will suffer. These writers continued the Jahwist's view minus the sense of grace.

The Priestly source was the last major compiler of the previous writers' works. Their concern is painfully obvious. They present a view of YHWH in the wilderness that causes him to appear far more concerned with how the people will worship him than with how they treat one another or how they will survive the wilderness. They overload the commandments with a disproportionate list of cultic demands.

The prophetic writings are genuine and represent a rich heritage of spirit persons who sensed the movement of God in history and wrote with power and style. These writings are the ones written by the prophets of Israel and Judah. Clearly missing from the prophetic books of the Jewish Scriptures is the book of Daniel. Jewish scholars are quite aware that the book is anachronistic fiction. They are amused that so many Christians believe it to be genuinely historical.

The last section of the books of the Old Covenant was called the later writings. They were an assemblage of writings that had accumulated over the years which the Jews read, but did not yet view as authoritative. When Jesus refers to "The Law and the Prophets" he is referring to the *Torah* and writings of the prophets. The remainder became Scripture after the fall of Jerusalem in 70 A.D. These *later writings* were a collection of wisdom literature, history, fiction, and fictionalized history. Each contributed either some moral/ethical idea or another value important to their culture.

When Jerusalem fell to Titus in 70 A.D. and the Temple was destroyed, the Jewish leaders fled to Joppa. They realized they were to begin another exile and decided to select and canonize the Scriptures they believed to be valid and helpful for their people. Rather than allowing the test of time to select the writings, they did so because they felt there was not enough time to allow for that. Also at that time, "heretical writings" were beginning to appear that claimed a false messiah had purportedly risen from the dead and was offering a new faith. Closing the canon for all time appeared to them to be the way to thwart this new, false religion called *The Way.*

The Jews never believed YHWH had dictated their scriptures. They merely were those writings which they believed had proved themselves to be valuable over the years. The careful, thoughtful scholar will acknowledge that any belief that the Holy Scriptures are the work of a single intellect is absurd. The most obvious example is to be found in 1 Samuel 16 and 17. There are two, radically different stories of how David entered Saul's camp and slew Goliath. There is no rational way to reconcile them. If one is correct the other must be wrong. There is another discrepancy that is difficult to track down. 2 Samuel 21 lists some of David's mighty men. Verses 18 -22 read:

> *Some time later when war broke out again in Gob; it was then that Sibbecha of Hushah killed Saph, a descendent of the Rephraim. In another war with the Philistines in Gob,* ***Elhanan son of Jair of Bethlehem killed Goliath of Gath****, whose spear had a shaft like a weaver's beam. In yet another war in Gath there appeared a giant with six fingers on each hand and six toes on each foot; twenty four in all. He, too, was descended from the Rephaim; and when he defied Israel, Jonathon, son of David's brother Shimeai killed him. These four giants were the descendants of the Rephraim in Gather, and they all fell at the hands of David and his men. (my bold type)*

When I first encountered that passage decades ago I was reminded of headlines during WWII that proclaimed: "Patton beats Rommel!" Patton and Rommel never physically confronted one another, of course. It was Patton's army that defeated Rommel's. Just as the passage of scripture read, "they all fell at the hands of David and his men." Out of this, a marvelous legend grew that had as much substance as George Washington maliciously chopping down a prized cherry tree. I would suggest that those who are interested in the entire David story read both the story found in Samuel and the story found in Chronicles. They are two, different accounts. One seems to be pro-King and the other is less favorable to him. Both cannot be true.

For a moment, think along with me on the issue of all Scripture being the divinely inspired, inerrant Word of God. I believe there is much of great value to be found in both the books of the Old Covenant and the books of the New Covenant. Finding these gems is somewhat like mining for gold, however. You have to be able to discern what is of value and what is not. You also must know where to look and have the patience to work through much that has no value at all. When asked what was the greatest commandment, Jesus responded that we should love the Lord our God with all our heart, soul, strength, and mind and our neighbor as ourselves. Then he added that on those two hung the law and the prophets, which essentially included their entire Bible at the time (Matthew 22:37-40).

When you sift through the Jewish Scriptures carefully you find that rich vein of truth running through them. Having said that, let's move on to examine this claim of inerrancy: I have read of innumerable attempts to prove the existence of Noah's Ark as though its mere existence would prove something of value for spiritual pilgrims. The question of whether there was a flood and an ark is irrelevant. The question is this: "Did the event occur *precisely* as described in Scripture?" If it did, then it supports the theory of inerrancy. If it did not, then it negates that theory. The ark was approximately 150 yards long, 25 yards wide and 15 yards high. It has been described a being like a three story building. Now, let's examine the cargo: Genesis 7:14-16 claims that God ordered Noah to put every life form onto the ark. I must assume that God also told Noah to bring the necessary seed for replanting all that the flood would destroy so we must account for that, as well. When I try to envision the task of doing that my mind begins to see a marvelous comedy (please indulge me): "Penguins! Where are the penguins? Don't forget the polar bears while you're there. Oh and speaking of bears, round up a couple of black ones and a couple of brown ones while you're at it. Shem, run over and pick up some lions, tigers, leopards, cheetahs – and, oh yes, we need two rhinos, two zebras, two elands" – "What an eland?" "I don't know, they look something like deer. Oh, that's right, Jepheth, get two deer and two moose and a couple of caribou and some buffalo. Let's see: we'll also need some monkeys, apes, gorillas. Did I mention hippopotamuses (or is it hippopotami?)?" He turns to his wife, "Honey, I hate to ask you to do this, but can you round up the snakes? You know how I am with snakes. Watch out for the cobras, rattlers and coral snakes. I'll go for the spiders. Tell your daughters-in-law to start collecting seed for the gardens and fields. Get the vegetables: carrots, beans, peas, broccoli" "Broccoli?" "Yes, honey, broccoli. It's good for you." At a certain point, Noah would remember that he has to provide food for all the animals – not only for during the flood, but until the animals and grain and vegetables and fruits grow. Then he realizes what he will need during the forty days, so he calls out to Shem: "Get some shovels – large, flat shovels. Eight shovels. We're going to be awfully busy for a while!"

Can I stop here? Do you see the total absurdity of the story? If the entire world was destroyed in a flood then every species of animal, bird, snake, insect, etc. would have had to be on that ark. That ark could have been as huge as the Queen Mary and still have been too small.[15] Additionally, the task of rounding up every life form on earth would have required a far greater technology and logistical capability than exists even today. I do not doubt there was a flood. The Babylonian flood story testifies to that. Whenever a vast area of land is flooded it undoubtedly appears to those in the flood that the entire world is flooded. Werner Keller, in his book, *The Bible as History*, presents evidence of a great flood in the Mesopotamian area and offers a rational explanation of the flood stories arising from them. However, either the Great Flood happened as Scripture recorded it, or it did not. *Either Scripture is iner-*

15 Scientists estimate that there are 8,000-10,000 different species of snakes and birds. Additionally, they estimate there are more than three million different species of all other living creatures.

rant in every detail or it is not. If it is not, then it becomes a matter of opinion which Scripture is true and which is not.

I will bypass the Exodus, but I will give this much for those who wish to pursue it. According to Exodus 12:37-38, there were 600,000 men plus their families, plus large herds of cattle plus flocks.[16] Since the pharaoh had ordered all male babies to be slain at birth we must assume that the number of women outnumbered the number of men. Let's say two to one. Then we add the children. Let's make that one per wife, so we have about three million people plus herds of cattle and flocks of sheep and goats. They said "large herds," so we will just add another million live beings. Try moving a total of four million people and animals on foot – anywhere. When it came to Moses striking the rock and producing water for all the travelers (Exodus 17:1-7) we have a logistical problem. If each person and animal required only two quarts of water in the arid desert heat to avoid severe dehydration, that would have been two million gallons. The water could have been gushing forth with more force than a fireman's hose and never approached the needed figure. Again, Keller's *The Bible as History* offers both eyewitnesses and archeological evidence of the Exodus as it probably actually occurred in history.

Christian Scriptures

The Christian Church gave birth to its Scriptures. Scriptures did not give birth to the Christian Church. For the first three hundred and fifty years of its history the Church operated without any authoritative Scripture. The Twelve Apostles plus the many other original disciples were the catalysts and guides for the first century. The writings of the martyrs added to this collection of leaders in the following centuries. As the church became more universally organized, new leaders arose to guide the still-budding faith through those perilous times. With the establishment of Christianity as the official religion of the newly consolidated Roman Empire under Constantine, the issue of authoritative order became a priority. Prior to that time, however,

16 Archeologists believe the actual number departing Egypt was much smaller.

there were notable scholars who focused their attention on the proper means of reading and evaluating the various writings that were being used by the churches. Most notable among the early scholars was a young Alexandrian named Origen. He delved beneath the literal meaning of Scripture to search for allegorical, moral and spiritual thoughts that he believed lay beneath the surface. In some regards he was the first genuine biblical scholar. His brilliance promoted him to become the head of the Alexandrian School when he was but eighteen years of age.

Responsible Biblical scholarship is not a simple matter of memorizing Scripture and/or learning what earlier scholars have written about it. Reputable scholars take responsibility for what they teach. In order to do this, the contemporary scholars must do their own research. Genuine scholars must learn the original language of the manuscripts, and be able to understand what those words would have meant to the people of that time. They must be able to distinguish between writing styles in order to ascertain continuity of authorship, and they must be willing to read either many seemingly duplicate manuscripts or at the least the research of those who have read them in order to understand and deal with the variations they contain. When this is finished, genuine scholars will understand that the writings of the early church were not considered authoritative until the end of the 4th century.

There are many examples that testify to the fact that the Scriptures are neither infallible nor divinely dictated. Scholars and careful, thoughtful readers will have encountered overwhelming evidence that the scribes who copied the Scriptures made additions and errors that often make it impossible to be absolutely certain what the original texts may have said. My original Greek New Testament, for example, often has as many footnotes on a page as actual text. The footnotes show the variations in texts from other manuscripts. Many writings had additions added by pious scribes who were merely trying to update these documents with what they believed to be factual material. A large variety of writings were read and used by early congregations. They were considered to be instructive guidelines – nothing more. As vastly different understandings of the faith began to appear, a concern arose for some form of unanimity, lest the Christian faith simply disintegrate into a multitude of heresies.

The earliest recorded concern was caused by the teachings of a ship owner and merchant named Marcion. He arrived in Rome circa 144 A.D., gave a generous gift to the church and began to teach his brand of Christianity. Marcion believed the deity presented in the books of the Old Testament was a lesser god, and Jesus was sent by the Ultimate Deity to correct his errors. Consequently his personal canon was the Gospel of Luke and the writings of Paul, expurgated of their Jewish influence. Because he taught in Rome, his teaching caught the attention of the early leaders of the Church. They began to question which of the many, many writings were authentic and worthy of being used as guidelines for the faith.

The list of acceptable writings quickly narrowed to less than forty. From there some of the more notable theologians, such as Origen of Alexandria, narrowed the list to about thirty. Irenaeus, bishop of Lyons, stated that there should be but four gospel accounts, giving as his reason the fact that there were but four major directions: east, west, south and north. This writer believes he had quite another agenda. I would note, however, that the four major directions do exactly that: they point in four different directions. I would think that a person could find a better analogy than suggesting the Gospel can be valid if they point the readers in different directions. Irenaeus also stated that the Gospels should be the accounts of eyewitnesses. In retrospect this seems not to have been followed since neither Mark nor Luke could make that claim. Later scholarship has demonstrated that neither Matthew nor Luke seems to have been eyewitness. Both follow the outline of Mark, which, according to Bishop Papias was his constructed chronology.[17] Also, we know a great deal about Simon Peter because the story told by Mark (and copied by Matthew and Luke) is Simon Peter's story. We know nothing about either Matthew or Luke, because it is not their story and they were not in it. Actually, Mark has the best claim because Bishop Papias stated that Mark had recorded the memoirs of his uncle, Simon Peter. It should be remembered in this regard that none of the Gospel accounts originally bore the name of their author. It was tradition, and only tradition, that gave each

17 Papias of Hieropolis is quoted by Eusebius, who in turn cites John the Elder. Papias was a contemporary of the disciples of the Twelve Apostles. Although none of his original writings remain, he obviously was the source of much that was recorded by many of the early church writers.

a distinctive name. The lack of a rational foundation for the selection is further highlighted by the fact that Thomas was an actual eyewitness to Jesus' life, death and resurrection, but was never considered for inclusion. Anyone working as a scholar in history must always be mindful of the simple fact that all writers – inspired or not – are human beings. We have our perspectives, biases and agendas. The list of authoritative written witnesses finally was that which we now call the books of the New Testament. In 367 A.D., Bishop Athanasius, often called the defender of Orthodoxy, issued a letter listing the twenty-seven writings in the New Testament canon. The Council of Carthage, 397 A.D. proclaimed those writings as canonical.[18]

Eventually all of the canonized Scriptures were organized into a single book. The book was named for the ancient Phoenician city of Byblos, known for its outstanding library. They did this quite conscious that what was assembled was for them a holy library that was made up of a mixture of history, historical fiction, fiction, poetry, prophetic writings, wisdom literature, myths, legends and miscellaneous writings. There was no thought of the writings actually being the "Word of God," or that all were historically true. They simply were writings believed to be inspired and worthy of instruction for the spiritual seekers, as we find in Timothy 3:16. Inspired (literally *God-breathed*) is not the same as God-dictated. We believe the prophets were inspired, but some of them were inaccurate in details.[19]

As earlier stated, for the first few centuries, the books we now call Scripture were considered just writings. There was nothing special or holy about them. Therefore scribes felt free to add to or edit them. One of the most flagrant examples of a later insertion is found in Mark. A typical translation of Mark starts with, "Here begins the good news of Jesus Christ, the

---

18 The Synod of Hippo Regius, 393 A.D., in North Africa is thought to have been the first Official declaration of Scripture as canon. However, all records of that synod were lost. The Council of Carthage in 397 A.D. is the authoritative source of the Western canon.

19 The prophet Micah predicted that Jerusalem would fall to Assyria. He was accurate in his assessment of the corruption that weakened the city, but failed to foresee that the Assyrians would mysteriously withdraw their siege of the city and move elsewhere. History is filled with people who have been inspired, *e.g.* artists, writers, composers. They have contributed greatly to our culture. I doubt, however, that God actually designed their creations. Words do change their meaning over a course of time. Religious fundamentalists have worked to change this term to be the equivalent of dictated. This never was the original meaning of the term, however.

Son of God." Those who possess later translations will find footnotes and perhaps different wording. Some early footnotes will say, "Some early witnesses omit 'Son of God.'" Others may simply read, "Here begins the good news of Jesus Christ" and add a footnote that says, "Some witnesses add 'Son of God.'" Some will say "a Son of God." I have not found one that properly states the correct translation. The background for this confusion is complex: Scribes were not required to understand Greek. They had only to demonstrate the ability to copy it correctly in order to be certified as scribes. Although both Matthew and Luke had a copy of Mark before them when they wrote, the church's understanding of Jesus as a spirit-filled man had evolved to a belief that he was, in fact, the child of Mary and the Holy Spirit. Therefore Jesus was for them the Son of God. A later scribe (no 1st century copy of Mark exists) thought it necessary to update Mark's account by adding this understanding to the introduction. He obviously did not read Greek well enough to understand the rules of grammar, so he merely copied the Centurion's statement made at the time of the crucifixion, not realizing it literally stated, "This man was a son of a god." Neither the Greek term *hious (son)* or *theous (of God)* had the preceding definite article. With the development of better scholarship theologians were able to determine that the statement, "The Son of God" in Mark's introduction was a later insertion.

The writings of Paul of Tarsus are the earliest of the New Testament accounts. These writings are unabashedly Paul's personal experience and understandings of the Risen Christ who encountered him. Paul was a key figure in the movement of the followers of the Galilean from a Jewish sect to a world religion. He was not the only person involved in spreading the message to the Hellenistic world, but his writings are the only written witnesses we have of that time frame. Too many Christians (clergy and laity) neglect to realize that Paul's letters were written to specific congregations to deal with specific issues of that congregation. He never intended these letters to become legal demands for all Christians. He was a first century pastor ministering to the needs of his people. No more. No less.

Were his writings inspired? I believe they were. Were they eternal truths and dictates? No. Paul of Tarsus shared *his first century vision*, *his first century understanding* of the Risen Christ. We are enriched by his writings. However, everything we know about Paul suggests that he never thought of his words as expressing eternal truths. He was fully aware that he was not God's Christ. Unfortunately, too many Christians cannot make that distinction. They ascribe the same authority to Paul's words as they do to the words of Jesus. It was Paul who cautioned that each of us must work out our own salvation in fear and in trembling. (Philippians 2:12) This necessarily requires developing our own understanding of Jesus, using whatever resources are available to us in doing so.

Some confusion over the relative merits of various Scriptures lies in the gradual distortion by worship liturgists. Once the canon was established and the selected Scriptures became authoritative, the early church stood when the Gospel accounts were read. They did this to emulate the tradition of people standing whenever a proclamation from the king was read. Simply stated they believed that Jesus was king and deserved the same respect. In most churches today the liturgists call the people to stand when *any* of the Scriptures are read. Then the liturgist usually concludes the reading by holding the Bible high and saying, "The Word of God for the people of God." This conveys a totally non-historical, non-biblical understanding of the Scriptures that places the words of Leviticus on a par with the Sermon on the Mount. I believe every preacher since the council proclaimed the acceptable canon has developed his or her own personal canon. There are many books that I never have used for teaching or preaching. They simply never offered anything of value to me that I thought was worth passing along. Every preacher I know has acknowledged doing the same.

Summary

Any reputable biblical scholar has to know that our Scriptures are a compilation of many writers. Most of those who wrote them had no idea they would someday be considered infallible and authoritative. The decisions as to which books should have been selected to be considered authoritative was reached after years of struggle, research and prayer. When one considers the tools and communication available to them, they must be given credit for having done quite well. However, what we tend to have today are two camps: one places

Scripture as the highest authority. The other seeks to understand and obey the Risen Christ. It really is a matter of living either by the Law or in the Spirit.

Frankly, I do not understand why people spend their time trying to prove that some of the stories found in the book of Genesis are true. Jesus either is or is not the Christ of God, because of who he is to us who are alive today. An ancient flood does not make him real. Those who are seeking to find proof from the past cannot be the same people who experience the Risen Christ today. The Christian faith is vital only when those who profess it do so from experiential conviction. Anything else is secondhand faith.

Serious students of Scripture must learn to distinguish between myth, legend and reality. There are riches to be found in the writings but you must learn how to find them. Anyone – anyone at all – who claims Scriptural inerrancy, is not the person to teach you.

deist - rejects authority as
the source of God's power.
Belief in 1 God but
disenchanted w/ Biblical
inerrancy

Section Two

THEN AND NOW

It was the Age of the Enlightenment that introduced the emerging paradigm. In that respect, the Enlightenment also was the Age of Anti-Traditional Religion. I understand it as the culmination of the era that began in the 14th century with the Renaissance in Florence, Italy and eventually spread throughout Europe in other forms. The 16th century Protestant Reformation was its religious expression. Finally, in the late 17th and 18th centuries it blossomed into a cultural revolution that emphasized individualism and reason. Essentially, Western civilization broke the bonds of the Christian Church that had dictated what constituted truth and acceptable thinking for centuries. Isaac Newton had reshaped and redefined the entire universe, totally contradicting the universe proclaimed by Scripture. It was the age of Voltaire, John Locke and David Hume who chipped away at the intellectual foundations of Christendom. Many traditional Trinitarians became functional Deists. They continued to attend their churches, but they no longer believed in a deity who acted like a celestial puppet master, manipulating the physical laws of the universe in order to serve the needs of individuals or small groups of people. Isaac Newton had demonstrated the inflexibility of those laws of physics, established by the Creator God. They reasoned that a benevolent God had created the best of possible worlds and then left the world and its inhabitants to their own devices. Many of the founding fathers of our nation were Deists. Most notable among them were Thomas Jefferson, Benjamin Franklin, George Washington, James Madison and Thomas Paine.

They functioned as Christians in so far as they adhered to Christian principles and had great admiration for Jesus. However, their emerging scientific orientation could no longer accept the underlying theology. Unfortunately, in abandoning traditional religion they also inadvertently dismissed the idea and the realm of spirituality.

The Second Great Awakening of the last part of the 18th century was a bit of reaction to the sterile theology of Deism. It overflowed with emotion, drawing heavily upon the threat of hell fire and damnation for its converts. The seesaw between intellectual and emotional Christianity has been with us since that time.

Lost in the midst of these struggles was the realm of the spirit. By the time I had completed my seminary education I had learned to equate *spiritual* with *emotional.* In the highly intellectual atmosphere of the seminary in the 60's, spirituality was dismissed. It was during those years that the God is Dead movement erupted. The churches had been operating on the strong national religiosity of post WWII, but the energy of that had begun to fade. It also was about that time that we began to import Eastern spirituality to fill a felt need. Transcendental Meditation groups began forming, where the members would sit about chanting "Om," never realizing they were invoking a Hindu deity. The western mind, however, is not compatible with eastern thought, so this attempt soon faded. Some fine quality western minds, however, began pioneering a form of western spirituality that was compatible with the western psyche. Dr. John Biersdorf was one.[1] I had the good fortune to meet him in the early 70's while I was involved in my own search for a form of religion that would give depth and greater meaning to my life. Jack taught me the practice of Christian meditation and offered the missing pieces for my reconstruction of a theology that served mind, emotion and soul.

The ancient Greek philosophers believed the mind and soul were somewhat intertwined, but that it was the mind that could guide the soul. I happen to believe it is a two-way avenue. The rational part of the mind may guide the soul. However, it is the soul that has the final say as to how the mind will grow and develop. With the awareness that the ultimate goal is

---

1 Dr. John Biersdorf earned his PhD in Psychiatry and Religion. He still is active as a spiritual counselor in the greater Detroit area.

the soul – not the mind – I will proceed to explore the means of rethinking the doctrine of old to fit the needs of a modern mind.

The clearest method for speaking of the old paradigm versus the new is to examine each of the major doctrines separately: First the old, fading paradigm, then the new, emerging paradigm. I will present a brief history and analysis of the development of each doctrine as it evolved. Then I will offer some new interpretations I believe are consistent with the emerging paradigm. I do not claim them to be either accurate or authoritative. I offer them because they present alternative ways of interpreting long-held doctrines. Perhaps they will serve as a guide for rethinking your beliefs on these doctrines. They have aided me in working my way through a maze of theological contradictions and non-biblical beliefs to find a rational and workable relationship with the one Jesus simply called *Father*.

We shall examine them in this order:

God the Father
Jesus Christ
Holy Spirit
Creation and the Fall
Law (Torah)
Sin/Evil
Atonement
Grace
Prayer
Salvation
Heaven and Hell

There will necessarily be some redundancy, but that will serve to reinforce the explanations.

Chapter Eight

God the Father

To say that one believes in God is meaningless. James points that out when he says, "You believe that there is but one God. Good! Even the demons believe that – and shudder." (James 2:19) It is *what you believe about God* that is absolutely critical. *What you believe* shapes your faith. *What you believe* determines how you understand life and its purpose. *What you believe* establishes the values that you will attempt to live by and the goals you will strive to accomplish. Whenever I hear someone say, "What does it matter what we believe? We are all going to end up in the same place," I know I am listening to someone who mindlessly repeats pious phrases without ever considering what they mean. The prophets of the Jewish Bible constantly warned about worshiping false gods. They were not worried about losing members or someone using the wrong names in the prayers. Their concern was that false gods represented the wrong values and goals. The gods of the Canaanites, for example, represented sexuality and wealth. Much of our society today continues to place these values above that of the God of Abraham, Moses and Jesus. Many call themselves Jewish or Christian, but that is mere lip service. That which lays claim to their souls is not the nature, values or goals of YHWH. We even have self-styled "Christian" preachers today who proclaim that the God of Jesus wants them to be successful by the world's false standards, although this is antithetical to everything Jesus lived and proclaimed. That which you believe – genuinely believe deep within your soul - about God most certainly sets the course of your life's journey.

The Finite cannot define the Infinite in detail. That is simple logic. Anyone who claims to be able to fully define the nature and will of God has lost touch with reality and should be ignored . . . and possibly hospitalized. However, we can draw from the lessons of the past and our present life understanding and experience to make some reasonable assumptions.

The Christian understanding of Deity was shaped from the Jewish model that developed in the old paradigm when the Earth was considered the center of a tiny universe. The old paradigm presented a deity that was a confused blending of the Old Testament deity, YHWH, and the metaphysical deity of the Greeks. If you read the books of the Old Testament judicially, paying attention to the divine nature being presented, you have to be confused by the contradictions. That deity was the God of Abraham, Isaac and Jacob. He was the deity who called Noah to build the ark and then started the Great Flood. He was the author of the Ten Commandments, the One who led the Children of Israel out of Egypt. He also was blended with the Greek deity who was Omniscient, Omnipotent, and Omnipresent, unlike Ezekiel's deity who moved about on a chariot, He was everywhere at once. Yet He also was totally transcendent and unknowable. The Jewish God of Moses had forgotten about his people in Egypt (Exodus 2:24), sometimes regretted his decisions (Genesis 6:6) and even changed his mind about slaying the children of Israel after Moses told him of the consequences (Exodus 32:14). The Hellenistic deity knew everything that was, is and ever would be. He foresaw all history laid out in a pattern and was aware of everything that ever would happen. He also was a greatly improved version of the deity who had to try, try and try again to get Pharaoh to let his people go. Nothing was impossible for this Greek deity. Eventually this blended deity assumed the character of a celestial Santa Claus. He knew if you had been naughty or nice, and dispensed punishments and rewards accordingly. He also was some kind of a puppet master who controlled the events of humanity.

The Jewish deity began as a tribal god, or actually a collection of tribal gods. Biblical scholarship has revealed that the deity of Abraham and Judah was known as YHWH, commonly called Yahweh. When translated it usually is written *I AM*. The deity of Jacob and the tribes of Israel were called

Elohim. When translated into English, Yahweh becomes God, and Elohim is *The Lord God*. The casual reader never suspects that these represent two different deities, and the early editors of the Hebrew Scriptures do a fine job of blending them. El Shaddai is another term and is translated as *God Almighty*. As the various tribes gathered into a single community the names became somewhat interchangeable in referring to their now-single deity. It remained for the Unknown Prophet of the Exile, often called 2nd Isaiah, to boldly proclaim there was but a single God of all Creation (Isaiah 46:6-8, 45:5, 21-22). This writing is dated somewhere around 550 B.C.E. The God of Joshua, Samson, David and Solomon did not behave as the God of all people. Rather, he seemed to delight in slaying any of his subjects who opposed the Hebrews. At the time of Jesus Yahweh was perceived as legalistic and requiring sacrifices in atonement for wrong actions. Jesus attempted to change this understanding in the people's minds. He renamed Yahweh, *Father,* and defined him as loving and forgiving. This was quickly lost as the church spread outside of its Jewish roots into the Hellenistic world. At that time the Greek deity began to merge with the Jewish, as mentioned earlier. The sense of the immediacy of God was displaced and priests again became necessary as intermediaries between humanity and deity. Once again, Yahweh was perceived as legalistic and demanding some form of sacrifice as atonement for wrong deeds. The Protestant Reformation only reinforced this understanding. Martin Luther, a church history scholar, realized that the early church had no prescribed prayer of confession. He removed it from his liturgy, calling it "a man-made instrument of the Devil," because he intuitively understood its destructive qualities. However, Luther was so addicted to guilt that he quietly reinstated it, like some alcoholic sneaking a bottle back into his house. Calvinism, that quickly became the dominant theology, emphasized the doctrine of Predestination, in which one is considered to have been predestined for either Heaven or Hell, and nothing could be done to change that designation. An arbitrary deity had determined the eternal fate of each one of his creatures, and one could only accept it. If believers bothered to explore this theology in depth, they would have seen how foolish and self-destructive it was. If your eternal fate is sealed at your birth then your behavior has no effect on it. You either are one of the blessed or one of the damned - period! No action – no change of mind or heart - can alter your eternal destiny.

Whatever you do throughout your life will either be pleasing or displeasing to God, so you might as well do what pleases *you.*

That was the logic. The reality, because of human egocentricity, was quite the opposite. Earlier I mentioned how that concept of predestination evolved into the work ethic and then into the spirit of capitalism. For the same reason, the Calvinists worked at becoming what they believed to be the ideal ethical person. This would prove to themselves that they were one of "the chosen." Like the Pharisees of Jesus' time, they set severe rules of behavior and then struggled to follow those rules.

The de facto deity of many self-proclaimed Christians today more nearly resembles the legalistic, vengeful deity of the Old Testament than the loving, redemptive and liberating deity that Jesus called *Father.* As mentioned earlier, the deity we proclaim arises from our own experience – not that of others. Some wise observers have noted that the rigid, fundamentalists of Islam, Judaism and Christianity are more spiritually akin to one another than they are to all other members of their own proclaimed faith. They insist on interpreting the writings of their faith in legalistic terms, rather than as statements of a philosophy that guides but does not need to control. They are judgmental, emphasizing punishment rather than forgiveness and redemption. The reality of who we are at our core supersedes any other claims.

As Joshua offered prior to crossing the Jordan, "Chose this day whom you will serve." (Joshua 24:15) I suggest you use this time of working your way through this book to do the same. ***It is not the name of a god but the qualities of that god that lay claim to your soul and determine the way your soul will develop.***

Now

In a universe that extends nearly fourteen billion years in time and space the image of the Grand Old Man in the Sky simply is untenable for the mind grounded in the scientific paradigm. It is inconceivable that any human-like individual, no matter how powerful or intelligent, could create and maintain such an immense, ever-changing universe. Further, the intelligence has to be of a totally different nature than that of humans.

Think along with me for a moment as, together, we magnify the image of God from a deity atop of a mountain to the creator of what now is our known universe. Light moves at approximately 186,000 miles per second. The light from our sun travels the 93 million miles in just over eight minutes. Try to envision how far that light would travel in an entire year: approximately seven trillion miles. That is one light year. Multiply that one year's distance by 14 billion (98 plus 21 zeroes). *That* is the size of our present known world. Scientists have established that the rate of acceleration of this universe is increasing and there is no foreseeable end to it. Further, the universe is expanding into sheer nothingness, creating both time and space as it does so.

At this point frankly my words have outrun my mind. I can write or say these words but their actual meaning escapes me. My mind was not designed to think in terms of billions of trillions or beyond a realm of time and space. I only believe such a realm exists because it is the only explanation I am capable of imagining. When we speak of God today we are speaking of an unimaginable mystery. Yet, even as my mind totters on the brink of overwhelming wonder and confusion I hear within myself – or perhaps I simply gain an understanding – that says, "Nevertheless, my son, I am with you and within you."

Although we must admit that fully comprehending this Creator/Sustainer of this universe is far beyond our ability, Christians should take seriously the statement of Jesus that those who have seen him – who have looked beyond the external to grasp his nature – have also seen the Father. For Christians, Jesus is the means by which we are able to see and understand what we are capable of understanding about the nature and will of the One we call God.

This requires a radical departure from the image too often depicted in the books of the Old Testament (Covenant).[2] Jeremiah proclaimed to the people that they had broken their covenant with God, and the new covenant would be written, not on stone, but in their hearts. At his final supper with

2 The Greek *entole* translates as *covenant* or *testament*. *Christians are not bound by the laws of the Old Covenant*. They are called to live in the *spirit* of the *New Covenant*.

his disciples Jesus proclaimed that as the first covenant had been sealed with the blood of a lamb, so the new covenant was sealed with his blood. (Mark 14:24) In Matthew 5:17, Jesus said he did not come to break the old Law of Moses, but to bring it to fulfillment. He dug beneath the legalism of literal meanings to reveal the underlying basis and the spirit that gave rise to the words. Jeremiah tells the people of the new covenant that God will make with them when they return from exile:

This is the covenant I will make with the house of Israel in those days: I will put my law in their minds and write it on their hearts and they shall be my people and I shall be their God (Jeremiah 31:33).

The Unknown Prophet of the Exile said God had called them to be a light to nations that His salvation might be known to the end of the earth. (Isaiah 49:6) However, Ezra ignored Jeremiah's call for the people to take foreign wives and live peacefully and productively in the land of their exile. He instructed the men in Jerusalem to rid themselves of foreign wives or be exiled to Samaria (Ezra 10:10). He effectively constructed a wall around Israel instead of opening the doors to become that light to the nations. As a consequence, many believed the new covenant remained only an unfulfilled promise until Jesus and his followers opened those doors to the world. Christians live by the New Covenant. They are not bound by the old. The laws of Leviticus have no hold on them. They eat pork. They are not bound by Sabbath laws. Those of the new paradigm, who continue in the ways of Christ, come to understand the truth and are set free. Their Heavenly Father never intended them to become prisoners of meaningless and debilitating demands. When called to account for picking grain to eat on the Sabbath Jesus responded, "The Sabbath was made for humanity, not humanity for the Sabbath." (Mark 2:27).

In no way, however, is this intended to suggest there are not demands on our lives, or that our actions have no consequences. I am simply stating the obvious: the path of growing as followers of Jesus is not the same as that of a faithful Jew who abides by the covenant of Mt. Sinai. I firmly believe that we are as fully capable of experiencing ourselves living in the presence of God as those figures of old: Abraham, Moses, Peter, Paul or any other figure of note. Those we think of as saints or prophets were essentially no different than we. There was no magical era in which God broke some invisible barrier to reveal himself more fully. There have been individuals, in every generation, who were open to the presence of God in whom we all "live and move and have our being," as Paul said in Acts 17:28.

Every generation since humans have been walking the earth has known those individuals who were sensitive to the presence of the divine. They have been called shamans, medicine men, seers, prophets, spirit persons, psychics, mystics, and an assortment of less favorable names. Most people I know have had some form of transcendent moments, but dismissed, forgot them, or neglected to reflect upon them. Yet, they continue to pray to a deity they believe can hear and respond.

I want to propose a radical way of conceptualizing that which we call God. I would refer you to Psalm 139:7 where the psalmist asks, "Where can I go from your Spirit? Where can I flee from your Presence?" For that writer, God's Presence and God's Spirit are identical. Jesus' only definition of God's quality of existence is the one in John 4:24 where he says "God is Spirit." We speak of God as Omnipresent, but rarely consider what that implies: *everywhere at once*. While watching a video dealing with dark energy and dark matter, a few related facts drew together in my mind

1. Neither matter nor energy can be created nor destroyed. We may convert one from the other. Matter is just condensed energy. We know even the most solid appearing items are masses of molecules comprised of atoms that are constantly in motion. Matter is condensed energy.

2. We live in a constantly increasingly expanding universe. The entire universe is greater today than it was yesterday, and it will be even larger tomorrow.

3. Dark energy and dark matter are not proven entities. They are theoretical constructs to explain how the mathematics of astronomy function. In order for the math to work, the mass of the universe must be enormously greater than it is. Since the math does work, the assumption is that approximately 97-98% of the universe is invisible and unknowable to us.

As these fell together in my mind the thought occurred to me that what the scientists are conjecturing as *dark energy* and *dark matter* might be what religionists have been calling YHWH, Brahman, Allah, and God for centuries. Paul had intuitively spoken of God as one "in whom we live and move and have our being."(Acts 17:28) We cannot experience this Spirit physically simply because *we are not designed to experience deity in that way.* We must encounter, experience, worship and commune with God as Spirit. "God is Spirit, and those who worship Him must do so in spirit and in truth."(John 4:24). We are not physical beings who occasionally may have a spiritual experience. We are spiritual beings who presently are undergoing a physical experience. Whether or not you accept this understanding, today's paradigm calls for us to dismiss the man-in-the-sky and begin to conceptualize God as an ever-present reality who is everywhere at once. To me, that can only mean *Spirit.*

Points to Ponder

Although we may feel comfortable thinking of God in anthropomorphic terms, we really need to drop that model if we are to imagine the scope and power of the one we call God. In my private prayers I never speak aloud. There is no need. I sometimes recall a scene from *0 God*, when George Burns was portraying God in the flesh. He was asked, "Do you really hear all of our prayers?" His reply was, "I hear them. I don't always listen." For me, communication with our Heavenly Father transcends words. None are required for understanding. When we image the nature of God we really should decide if God is a loving, redemptive and empowering deity with whom we can entrust our most secret inner self, or if God is more distant, more judgmental. We also should determine whether we consider God to be one who manipulates the events of the world, or if God has created a world for us that best suits his desires for how we can grow spiritually while living within it.

Another aspect to be considered is whether there is pure monotheism or if more than one divine deity exists. Amos poses a rhetorical question: "Does evil befall a city unless the Lord has done it?" (Amos 3:6). Prior to the introduction of Persian dualism YHWH was considered the author of everything – both good and evil. We either live in a universe entirely governed by a single deity or we have two or more deities competing with one another. There is no middle ground. Medieval theologians discussed the limits of God's power, sometimes to the point of absurdity. Yet that question needs some kind of response by those who would worship God. If you genuinely desire to place your life in God's hands you should have some concept of the limits and extent of God's power.

Chapter Nine

Jesus of Nazareth

Scripture makes it quite clear that there was no single doctrine of the nature and purpose of Jesus of Nazareth. Each writer presents a different understanding of his nature and his mission. I ask you to set aside any understanding you have of the nature of Jesus as you read these various interpretations. Then using Wesley's quadrilateral, formulate your own understanding.

One simple but significant factor in what I call the *Deification of Jesus*, is the cultural process by which he finally was thought of as God-in-the-flesh. The two major religions competing with Christianity both claimed full-fledged gods as their leaders and objects of worship. Roman emperors were declared to be gods. Emperor worship was one of the religions of the Empire. A letter written by Pliny the Younger to Trajan, the second century emperor of Rome, told of Pliny's observations of Christians: ". . . they were accustomed to meet on a fixed day before dawn, and sing a responsive hymn to Christ as a god." Trajan replied, telling Pliny not to seek them out, but if they were identified as Christians to allow them to prove their loyalty by making a sacrifice to the emperor as a god. When the Christians refused to make the required sacrifice they gave their reason as only worshiping one god. Then they were asked why they worshiped two gods: Yahweh and Jesus of Nazareth. This was one reason for the Greek theologians to begin wrestling with the problem that eventually ended up as a Trinitarian doctrine: Father, Son *and* Holy Spirit.

The rest of the process is a bit more complex:

The earliest Gospel, Mark, clearly demonstrates that the followers of Jesus thought of him as totally human.[3] When they finally saw him as the Christ (Anointed One) of God they still did not see him as other than a man (Mark 8:27-30). Yet, upon experiencing his resurrection they abandoned all fear of death and devoted their lives to spreading his message. The Jerusalem Church and Antioch never claimed him to be more than a man. The terms they used for him were either "Christ" (Hebrew "Messiah") which meant *Anointed One*, [4] or the one he employed to speak of himself: *The Son of Man* or Second Adam who came to repair the damage caused by the first Adam's disobedience. When speaking of Jesus' accomplishments Paul specifically mentions that he was obedient to the death. (Philippians 10:10). You have read the explanations of Jesus' evolution from human to deity. There were pressures to explain monotheistic claims, competition from other religions with full-fledged gods. There also was a need to explain the process by which loyal followers become immortal. None of these issues exist today.

I find the Jesus presented by Mark to be a compelling person. He was an ordinary man from an ordinary family. However, he possessed an extraordinarily keen and insightful mind. He was one of those rare persons that Marcus Borg defines as a "spirit person," as much in touch with - and at home in – the spiritual realm as the physical. He did not accept superficial, surface answers to life's questions. He was possessed of a generosity of spirit that was able to focus upon and genuinely understand the people he contacted. There was no drifting of mind, loss of focus, as with us whose minds wander as others try to connect to us. When caught off guard at a bad moment, he lashed back at the Syro-Phoenician woman (Mark 7:24-30). However, her response brought out his better self and he healed her daughter. The Jesus revealed in this brief event is a great model for those of us who spout out deeply embedded prejudices in moments of stress! Mark's Jesus comes to the Jordan, not really knowing what he seeks, but at the moment of baptism he has an overpowering vision that he is being adopted by Yahweh as his son.

3 Mark 1:1 has footnotes that explain in varied ways that "The Son of God" is a later addition {see Section on Scripture).

4 Jewish kings were anointed, not crowned.

As with many earlier cultures he goes to the desert to fast and await an understanding of his life's purpose and design. I believe it is not until his time in Caesarea Philippi that he fully understood that his mission would end on the cross. Even on his last night, in the Garden of Gethsemane, he sought to avoid that (Mark 14:32-36). There was no written guarantee of a resurrection. He only had a deep-seated trust in the quiet voice within himself that the cross was not the end of him and everything he had given his life to attain. The reflective reader will note that Mark's Jesus never gives an explanation of the meaning of his death. At the last supper he does not even suggest it is for some form of atonement (Mark 14:22-25).

It is impossible to reconcile Matthew's birth narrative with that of Luke. One begins in Nazareth. The other occurs entirely in Bethlehem, and the family is found dwelling there in a house more than a year later. That does not present a problem for me. Myths and legends arise around famous people. Years ago I happened across an account of George Washington and the famous cherry tree incident that had been published within fifty years of Washington's death. To illustrate George's truthfulness he wrote, "It is said that young George once accidentally scarred his father's favorite fruit tree." This has evolved to maliciously chopping down a cherry tree. There was a gram of truth that had grown over time. This is natural, and scholars understand how to interpret it. Abe Lincoln has many similar stories attesting to his honesty. The fact that legends spread and endure tells us more than an historical truth possibly could. It reveals how the hero was perceived. Who would believe the birth narratives if they were ascribed to any other historic figure? People are saying that in the person of Jesus they experienced both the human and the divine. Even Mark expresses that idea with his Spirit-filled Jesus.

Luke's task in presenting the story of Jesus to a Roman citizenry was difficult and complex. He translated a Jewish event into Greek for a Hellenistic audience. Additionally, he had to persuade his audience that a Jew who had been condemned to death by Roman authority – and his followers – who also were considered outlaws - were the representatives of God who could redeem their lives and offer them eternal life. The careful reader notes that Pontius Pilate found no fault in Jesus, but approved his death as a matter of expediency. The centurion who sent Paul to Rome also expressed his belief that Paul was innocent of any wrongdoing. The parables written in Luke are precious stories in which Jesus speaks of the nature of God. Another theme that ran throughout Luke's account was that Jesus had a great concern for the poor and the outcast, and his message was for everyone. One would do well to concentrate on the words and actions of Jesus, the Christ of God, and give them priority over the writings of Paul, an inspired and dedicated 1st century man who never saw the human Jesus when he walked this earth. The same can be said for all other theologians who can only share their rich experiences of the Risen Christ.

John's account is the last of the Gospel writings in the canonical books. We have no idea of the authorship. Tradition alone has given its name. Matthew and Luke obviously had a copy of Mark before them when they wrote. Matthew's intended readership was Jewish and Luke's was Roman. John, however, had a different agenda and created an entirely different scenario. He ignored the early ministry and focused upon Jesus' time in Jerusalem. This has caused a few scholars to speculate that the author was a resident of Jerusalem. Be that as it may, his Jesus is entirely different from the other three Gospel authors. John viewed Jesus as the Divine Logos of God encased in human flesh. When John chose to use the term "flesh" he probably realized that the term carried the connotation of humanness. "The spirit is willing but the flesh is weak" (Matthew 25:41) is an example of this usage. John, along with the others, saw both the human and the divine in the person of Jesus. Each expressed it in different terms and in different proportions of humanity/divinity. Still, all stated the same basic idea: *in the person of Jesus a person experienced both the ideal human and the divine.*

There are questions I believe must be addressed by all who embrace the emerging paradigm and would be followers of this Man of Galilee. Genuine faith cannot be built upon blind belief. It must arise from Wesley's quadrilateral and be fully believed and trusted, or it is a secondhand faith that will fall apart in times of crisis. Genuine faith is not afraid of challenging long-held beliefs to see if they actually still seem valid.

At this point, I offer a functional definition of truth: *Truth is that hypothesis that successfully answers every question put to it.* When a new question arises that the hypothesis cannot satisfactorily answer then the hypothesis must be abandoned or revised until it fully answers that question. When the understanding of the world has changed so as to render those old questions meaningless, then new questions must be formulated to test the truthfulness of the hypothesis.

1. Is it necessary for Jesus to be divine for you to become his follower? If yes, why?

   I believe the contrary is true. The belief that Jesus was divine negated his ability to serve as an example to humanity. I have heard countless responses to the demand to be like Jesus dismissed by the words, "But he was divine. Don't ask me to do what he did."

2. Must Jesus be divine in order to serve as an example for humans? If yes, why?

   The answer to this is the same as for the previous question. One who is divine is immortal. Death held no more fear for him than volunteering to be sawed in half by a stage magician.

3. Does Jesus as divine help your understanding of the meaning of his death and resurrection, or would it have greater significance if he was human? Why?

   You must answer this question for yourself. Aside from the fact that this may have been a long-held, comfortable belief, what purpose does a divine messiah serve that could not be served by a human Jesus anointed by God? Since it was Jesus' resurrection that gave credence to his message that human life does not end with our physical death, does making him divine strengthen or weaken that message?

In teaching courses on World Religions I realized there was some value in every one. Each rose from its culture to present some understanding of ultimate deity, our human destiny and the paths others have found to bring them into some relationship with their understanding of God. Although the culture is quite different from ours I have found the religions of India helpful in interpreting the Scriptures. Their religions are ancient and more consistent with the culture of the Near East than our Western culture. The story of Buddha's birth is an interesting myth. It tells of the gods going to the highest level of heaven to implore one of those highest evolved souls to return to earth to help them find their way out of their misled lives. One volunteered and was reborn in a miraculous fashion. He was a prince, showered with luxury and insulated from the woes of the world. He matured and married. Then one day he observed three phenomena: old age, sickness and death. Now aware of these ills that fell on all humanity, the prince no longer could abide his privileged life. He silently bade farewell to his wife as she slept, climbed the palace wall and disappeared into the night. After years of searching, while sitting under a Bo tree, he experienced sudden insight and full understanding. Now, as the Enlightened One, (Buddha) he went about teaching the way to enlightened living.

The myth may sound absurd to the outsider, but I would ask how it compares in credibility with the Virgin Birth stories of Matthew and Luke? Both Matthew and Luke expressed their belief that Jesus of Nazareth was a blending of the human and the divine. The two tales are mutually exclusive. Matthew begins in Bethlehem where there is no census, no filled inn and no shepherds – only magi who arrived to the house in which they were living, more than a year later. Luke begins in Nazareth, but journeys to Bethlehem because the normally efficient Romans ordered an absurd method for conducting a census. Every male had to abandon his home and business in order to return to the place of his birth – where there were no birth records.[5] Neither story gives credence to our faith. Rather, it is our faith that allows one to accept the narratives.

It was the Council of Trent, held more than fifteen hundred years after the resurrection, where the decision was made to declare reincarnation a non-Christian teaching and a heresy. Actually, I find traces of belief in reincarnation in our New Testament scriptures. When Jesus asked his disciples who people thought he was, they answered in terms of reincarnation of past heroes (Mark 8:27-28). It is my belief that someone at the council finally realized the doctrine of reincarnation could put the church out of business. What purpose does it serve to offer eternal bliss *if the public knows they have to repeat this life?*

5 There are no records of a census being conducted prior to the attempt during the reign of Augustus Caesar.

We have heard the expression, "That person is an old soul." We have observed the differences in children. One seems to act like an old soul from infancy while another looks fresh and without a clue. Some highly educated and reputable professionals have done research in that area that makes a compelling case for reincarnation. Dr. Brian Weiss, a noted psychiatrist, has published some interesting case studies. What if – just, *What if* - Jesus of Nazareth was one of those old souls who had evolved far beyond the ordinary? John 8:58 has Jesus making an extraordinary statement: "Before Abraham was, I am." Perhaps Jesus was so thoroughly in touch with the divine spark of God within himself that he could make this statement. Is it more or less conceivable that his essence was that of an advanced soul, or that of the God of an enormous, still developing universe?

I would suggest that a thoughtful reading of the Gospel demonstrates that none of the original Twelve perceived Jesus to be other than human. By the time that Simon Peter made his declaration that Jesus was, in fact, God's messiah (or Christ) he and the others had been followers of Jesus for more than two years (Mark 8:29)

Now

In a democratic society where individuality is an important value, the concept of Jesus as fully human should be embraced. Resurrection is not reserved for divine beings, nor is the intervention of a divine being necessary to bring individuals into proper relationship with a deity. Each of us is called upon to "work out your own salvation in fear and trembling," as Paul calls us to do in Philippians 2:12. The new paradigm seeks to make the followers of Jesus more than passive sinners needing to be saved and redeemed. It seeks to draw those who would follow Jesus into a vital partnership with him in transforming society and empowering them to live their lives courageously and fully. To use an analogy drawn from the comics: Batman and the Lone Ranger could have been partners. Superman could not have been a partner with either. He could have an aide or assistant but never a partner. No one else could fly, leap tall buildings or see through walls. Jesus of Nazareth had no other assurance that his death on a cross would end in victory – except his total faith in the God whose presence he felt within himself. To think otherwise is to do him a disservice. The account of his struggle in the Garden of Gethsemane testifies to his humanity. "Nevertheless, not my will, but yours,"(Luke 22:42). This should also put to rest any thought that Jesus was God-in-the-Flesh, or for that matter, that he was equal to God.

God's Spirit (or *Presence*) resides in each of us and is capable of making us much more than we now are. We deny that possibility when we deify Jesus and make him different. Many who call themselves Christians prefer to do so because adoration is far easier and more comfortable than imitation.

Points to Ponder

What is your understanding of the man we call the anointed one of God (Christ/Messiah) but also call Son of God, God-made-flesh? They are mutually exclusive terms, yet they often are used interchangeably. A man can be admired and a model. A god may be adored and obeyed. A man may die. A god is immortal. The divine paradox, as many theologians call it, claims Jesus to be fully human and yet fully divine. That is akin to imagining a square circle or a finite infinity. Paradox is a useful term for avoiding a reasonable explanation. However, there is no rational way in which this paradox can be conceived. In my studies I saw that every attempt to explain this was eventually branded as a heresy by some council. This is the inevitable consequence of various theologians attempting to solve cultural problems by redefining the nature of Jesus. Some needed him to be human in order to make the resurrection meaningful. Others needed him to be divine in order to fulfill their culture's requirement for immortality.

In spite of all the rational arguments, there have been vital, faithful followers of Jesus in every generation who have held every conceivable belief about his human/divine nature. I never waste energy or time over this. I only ask others to allow me the right to have my opinion. With any model offered the believers still feel that in encountering Jesus they have met both the human and the divine.

Chapter Ten

The Holy Spirit

After years of concentrated study on this single issue, the great medieval theologian, Thomas Aquinas is said to have confessed, "The Holy Spirit remains a holy mystery." He had encountered too many different usages and contradictions to be able to reconcile and make clear sense of the term. I was relieved to learn of this admission by such a notable scholar, because I also had arrived at that conclusion.

According to Platonic thought Divinity was totally transcendent, unknowable by any direct means. With the Son perceived as divine and the Father long acknowledged as divine there was no means by which one could conceptualize experiencing the divine in one's life. Scripture, however, had offered a word to fit that need: *Spirit.* That became the term people could use when attempting to speak of the experience of the Divine in their lives. However, the only time Jesus defines the nature of God (John 4:24) he says, "God is Spirit, and they who worship him must worship him in spirit and in truth." I have heard and read some attempts to rationalize that statement to fit the classic Trinitarian doctrine. They were heroic and I applaud them for their ingenuity. However, the clear meaning of Jesus' statement is obvious: God *is* Spirit, therefore *the Holy Spirit is God.* When we speak of God as omnipresent today we certainly must be thinking of God as Spirit. Any alternative view would be difficult to explain.

As with the need to find Jesus equal to God, the Greek theologians overlooked Scripture to speak of the Holy Spirit as an entity separate from

The Father. In order to insure the primacy of The Son, their creedal formula states that the Spirit proceeded from the Son, even though the Gospel of Mark clearly presents Jesus as receiving his power through The Spirit. Additionally, according to Mark the Holy Spirit thrust – or shoved – Jesus into the wilderness. Matthew softens this and has Jesus led or guided by the Spirit, but Mark's account probably was the remembrance of Peter as told to him by Jesus.

After reading and hearing innumerable sermons I have come to the conclusion that the term Holy Spirit is used to signify three entirely different phenomena:

1. The sense of God's Presence in one's life.

2. The awakening of the spirit implanted within themselves.

3. The collective spirit of an organization.

When I speak of experiencing God's presence in my life that is precisely how I speak of it: *Presence.* I do not say Spirit. My God is an immediate reality. I sense God's presence as fully as I sense the presence of another person. "Surely the Presence of the Lord is in This Place. I can feel his mighty power and His grace," is not a meaningless hymn to me. It expresses my experience – my expectations. *Presence* speaks of God. *Spirit* speaks of something else.

The first time I felt the Presence of God was as a young artillery officer during the Korean War. After years of attending church I finally had heard a preacher who made God and Jesus real and relevant in my life. I was newly awakened and now longed to experience the reality of God in my life. I hung around the church (that's where God resided, I thought) hoping for an experience like Isaiah's (Isaiah 6:1-13). Nothing happened however. All that was accomplished was that I dusted the furniture and cleaned whatever litter had been overlooked. Then one evening, while sitting in my living room, reading a book, I was overwhelmed with a sense of having been engulfed by a powerful presence. Without a word being uttered I understood an unheard voice that communicated, "I have been here all the time. You just never were open to my Presence." The next time I was to have that experience of Presence again was on my first night in Korea, as I descended a path to my newly assigned unit. This time there was no message. Still, my mind called forth the words of the 23rd Psalm: "*Though I walk through the valley of the shadow of death I will fear no evil, for Thou art with me.*" I felt a calmness merely in knowing I was not alone.

1 Kings 19: 9-14 recounts the story of Elijah standing on a mountain where there was a strong wind, then an earthquake, then fire. God was not to be found in any of them. Rather, Elijah encountered God in a still, small voice that finally spoke to him. It is not in the spectacular, but in the commonplace where God is met. Openness, patience and silence seem to be key ingredients.

This is why I use the term Presence when speaking of the awareness of God in my life. It is God: present to me, present within me. I wish I could live with the continual feeling of God's Presence. Still, it is enough to know – to genuinely *know* - that He is with me every moment, every step of my journey. There are those who will believe me to be delusional. They are only saying they have not yet had that experience.

Scripture speaks of people receiving the Holy Spirit, but I suggest an alternative way of understanding the gift of the Spirit. Before I do so, however, I must say a few words about perspectives. We all are familiar with being able to see the sun rise in the east, slowly move across the sky and eventually settle in the west to end the day. We have been taught that it is not the sun that is moving, but our own planet Earth that is slowly rotating. Still, our minds continue to observe the sun being the object that is moving. Our mind deceives us simply because we are not able to experience all the dynamics involved. The slow rotation of Earth is unfelt. In a similar manner I believe people speak of receiving the Holy Spirit, while in fact the spirit has risen from within their unconscious into their conscious awareness. We do not expect that so we interpret the experience as we have been conditioned to do so. Read the Scriptures carefully and you will note that receipt of the Holy Spirit always *followed* the proclamation of the Good News of Jesus Christ. I can only understand this as occurring in one of two possible ways: either some force decides to bestow the Spirit indiscriminately upon the listeners, or some profound response within the listeners awakened a dormant spirit.

When I consider the options I am reminded of experiments in which a piece of fine crystal responds to a musical sound by vibrating and beginning to faintly reproduce the exact pitch of the sound. In the Creation Story found in the second chapter of Genesis we are told that God breathed into Adam to give him life. The Hebrew and Greek words for breath are also translated as *spirit.* God *inspirited* humanity, setting us humans apart from all other living creatures. I think of the creation stories as myths: not necessarily historically true, but attempting to tell what is believed to be a greater truth. I believe the formulators of the creation myths were attempting to make a statement about the nature of humanity: made in God's image and enlivened with God's spirit. Paul speaks of "not I but Christ who lives within me," (Galatians 2:20). Again, I believe Paul was expressing what for him was the most rational explanation for the power he found within himself, just as you and I watch the sun traverse the sky. He could not envision himself as a person of power. He had even changed his name from Saul to *Paulus* (*little* or *small*) after his confrontation with the Risen Christ. I also would raise the question of how the Twelve were able to accomplish such great feats in their first missionary trips mentioned in Mark 6:7. At this point there had been no mention of them receiving the Holy Spirit. In fact, Mark never mentions the disciples receiving the Spirit. It seems to have occurred naturally within them as they traveled with Jesus. Jesus sensed the power within them. He would not have sent them out to fail. The same can be said for the seventy that Luke reports being sent out by Jesus to perform great acts (Luke 10:1). There was no suggestion that Jesus empowered them with a spirit. For John, the spirit was breathed into the disciples in the upper room immediately after the resurrection (John 20:22). There was no later moment at Pentecost, as told by Luke in the second chapter of Acts.

Those of the Hindu faith believe a spark of divinity resides in every person. They greet one another with the term, "Namaste," which means, "The divinity within me greets the divinity within you." The Stoics of old also believed this. The nature of deity was contained in the Logos and within each person was some particle of that Logos. For years, many Christians have been attempting to express this with the phrase "Christ Consciousness."[6]

6 Christ Consciousness simply means awakening the divine spark within the individual.

When I speak of this phenomenon I usually say The Spirit of Christ rather than The Holy Spirit. I do so because that enlivening spirit is shaped and defined by all I understand about Jesus. I resonate to him and the reality of who he was. It is the awakening of the Christ Consciousness – the Image of God in which I have been created. As a practical matter I move in and out of that awareness and aliveness. The mundane events of daily living capture my attention and I drift away, only to be awakened again by an event or a statement – or a powerful memory of who I was meant to be. Then for a while – a too brief while – I am to be numbered among those alive in the spirit. John Wesley called this "backsliding." In this regard I am a prototypical Methodist in the Wesleyan tradition, I fear. It is the part of me that echoes Paul: *Brothers and sisters, I do not consider myself to have taken hold of it. But one thing I do: Forgetting what is behind and straining for what is ahead, I press on toward the goal to win the prize for which God has called me heavenward in Jesus Christ.* (Philippians 3:13)

This is probably the manner in which most of us will and should experience this dimension of spirit. We all are not meant to be religious zealots whose total focus is on being active servants of Christ. We have families to care for, work that keeps the society functioning, friends, activities and avocations that call for our time and attention, making us more complete human beings. Like the Minutemen of old, we will serve "on call" – or as needed cadre. Most of our waking hours will be spent as ordinary decent citizens trying to make the best of the raw material of life we are given.

This resonating to the Spirit of Christ that generates the feeling of being born anew or feeling alive in Christ is that second meaning of Holy Spirit. The oldest accepted doctrine of the Church is stated in the phrase, "Where the Spirit of the Lord is, there is the one true Church." Nothing is said about a building, a creed or a name. I believe we understand that God is everywhere, so obviously "The Spirit of the Lord" is referring to more than God's presence, or the Church also would be everywhere.

Many of you have had the experience of walking into a room filled with people and immediately picking up the mood of the room without regard to the faces or body language.

Sometimes it is tension; sometimes anger; sometimes joy. It is not a matter of observation. It is a *feeling.* Whatever is happening has generated enough energy to be felt by others. I have walked into churches where I have felt joy, and I have walked into some where I have sensed tension or despair – or worse. One Monday morning I received a call from a lady who had visited the worship celebration the previous day. She exclaimed that, "the spirit was almost palpable." I knew what she meant. It was a spirit generated by the congregation that seemed to cling to the walls. For me, this is one way in which I use the word *Spirit.* It is a force that seems greater than the sum of its parts. It energizes and lifts those who share it.

The source of this energy is the other – and primary way – in which I use the term *Spirit.*

When I read the baptism story found in Mark 1:9-11, I picture Jesus rising from the water after his baptism and experiencing the vision of God's spiritual presence engulfing him like a dove. (Watch a dove descend. It does not resemble a diving plane. Rather it settles down, upright with wings slowly fluttering. Any small creature underneath a descending pigeon would be *engulfed*). In that moment his personal spark of divinity was released – ignited – manifested (choose your favorite word). Just as each individual has varying degrees of physical and intellectual gifts and/or talents, so I believe we have varying degrees of spiritual gifts. Jesus was one of those *Spirit Persons* of whom Marcus Borg writes. His awakened spiritual self, however, far exceeded the norm. Remember that there is absolutely no credible evidence that Jesus of Nazareth possessed any special power until that moment of baptism and awakening to his special calling by God. Mark even speaks of his fellow townsmen as discounting him because they knew him as a child and young adult. For them, he was not a returning hero, but merely an ordinary mortal, one of their own making extraordinary claims of greatness (Mark 6:1-6).

There is no chosen group who will be the only ones to receive the Spirit. There are only those who are willing to open their minds and hearts to the awareness of the ever-present God in their lives. There are those few who will struggle to understand the Christ lurking beneath the words of Scripture. They have experienced him by actually living out his commands, and searching themselves in reflective prayer. This option is open to everyone.

Summary

For me, God is Spirit. I have no problem with that. This is how Jesus defined Him. This is how I experience Him. My God is not the anthropomorphic entity often depicted in art. When I speak or think of experiencing God's Presence I simply say *Presence.* Some of us are more sensitive to the presence of others and will feel this presence - perhaps more often – perhaps more intensely. Still, all people, because we carry a portion of the divine spirit within ourselves, may all be open to this experience.

For me, Jesus is a spirit-awakened human whose spiritual potential far exceeded that of ordinary people. The biblical evidence (ignored by early theologians) is overwhelming that Jesus never considered himself to be divine and/or equal to God in any way. I believe the awakening of the spirit within ourselves occurs when our minds transcend their normal boundaries and we *behold* the reality of Jesus, and experience the Risen Christ in all his fullness. It is not having the Spirit *descend* upon us. It is an *inner awakening.*

Holy Spirit is the term I use when we refer to the collective spirit of a group. "Where the Spirit of the Lord is, there is the one true Church." Some groups are empowered and guided by a spirit of anger or hate, some by greed, some by pleasure, some by fear. *Holy Spirit* for me represents that collective spirit we find in Jesus Christ. In order to avoid confusion and being misguided, one must learn to discern spirits.

Chapter Eleven

Creation and *The Fall*

These two concepts must be treated concurrently, for in the minds of many they are inseparable. Those who live fully within the old paradigm and consider Scripture to literally be the dictated word of God view the two Creation myths as one continuous account. God created this "very good" world. He gave Adam and Eve dominion over the world. Then He sat back and rested. All went well until Adam and Eve violated His command, which was not to eat of the fruit of the tree of knowledge. When they did that, they were exiled from Eden and forced to work in order to survive. This Fall from innocence or grace upset the entire order God had created and Creation itself became fallen: broken and filled with sin and evil. Death entered into Creation and humanity's days were severely limited. When each person's life on earth came to an end, the person's spirit would rest in Sheol in eternal slumber. It was a simple understanding, made more complex over the years by speculative theologians and world events. Persian dualism entered into the Jewish culture and a Devil, complete with Heaven and Hell replaced Sheol.

As a practical matter, Judaism has no doctrine of the Fall as a curse passed along to all generations. That idea is strictly a later Christian development. Consequently it seems unlikely that Jesus of Nazareth had that in mind when he decided to face Roman justice and die on a cross. It also is difficult to imagine a God who believed he had created an entire world that was "very good" (Genesis 1:31) allowing everything to be corrupted because of one person's failure. That does not say much for the quality of God's workmanship. Sin takes over. Sickness and death strike randomly at every creature. One must assume that the world as created was very fragile, indeed.

Do not be timid about analyzing Scripture in this manner. The One who brought all of Creation from nothingness is not afraid of being "found out." To the contrary, I believe the creative and sustaining force we call God relishes being discovered for all He is. When we step outside of the pious explanations taught to us in early childhood, one must logically draw conclusions that bring us nearer in understanding to our Heavenly Father.

Now

There is a distinct and significant difference between perceiving Scripture as an authoritative guide and viewing it as a divinely dictated, inerrant legal document. The attempt to force schools to teach Creationism is as pathetic and futile as the medieval church's claim that its faith was the queen of the sciences, and the condemnation of Galileo for his recognition that the Earth was not the center of the universe. There is nothing resembling logic that requires a would-be follower of Jesus of Nazareth to literally believe the creation myths of Genesis. Rather, it is the desperate need for certainty that causes these Creationists to cling to a hopelessly inane and outdated set of beliefs. They are not followers of a living Christ who empowers and guides them in this troubled world. Rather, they are worshippers of an ancient collection of books written by people who had no understanding of the extraordinary scope of God's Creation. Their stubborn adherence to beliefs that are totally discredited by modern science actually hurts their children. Practically every study on the subject of IQ and religious preference claims that children of religious conservatives score lower on IQ tests than the more liberal Christians and atheists. From my own somewhat limited research on IQ's I believe one's IQ is not static. I believe one's IQ scores can be affected by one's environment, education and willingness to work intellectually. One could take two young boys or two young girls who had the identical physical potential, then give the first proper training, while the other becomes a couch potato and the first will far outperform the other. That occurs regularly. So it is with intellectual development. Select two with identical intellectual potential. Open one's mind to explore and question while the other is encouraged to accept unexamined facts and not to ask questions, and the first student outperforms the second on IQ tests. The second part of those aforementioned studies is that Atheists outperform Christian liberals on those same IQ tests. I contend that this supports my thesis that the brighter, more contemporary young person of today finds traditional Christianity to be inconsistent with the new paradigm and cannot accept its doctrines. Remember that in the last 60 years the churches have failed miserably to keep pace with the growing population.

In considering the nature of God and Creation we have two initial choices:

1. The cosmos always existed. There was no Big Bang or "In the beginning." In light of what we now are able to understand about this constantly expanding universe this seems unlikely. Scientists are capable of reaching back into time to a moment just after the beginning of our known universe. They place the beginning back to almost fourteen billion years ago. To deny this is to ignore the work of thousands of trained scientists, many of them devout Christians, who have an expertise in areas totally foreign to most of us. To believe their findings are some sort of conspiracy is absurd. There was a beginning!

2. The cosmos was and continues to be created. All evidence points to that. This raises another set of choices: either the universe was created for a purpose or it was just a random happening that continues to expand aimlessly creating space as it roams.

There is no solid evidence for either. Whatever decision is made probably is based on a multiplicity of factors, *e.g.* life experience, personality, present situation. I assume that readers of this book have opted to believe there is a purpose to Creation. The next choice then is whether to believe the Creator is aware of and concerned for the individual creatures. Deists might choose to believe the Creator created as perfect a world as possible and left his creatures to work their own ways through their lives as best they could. Actually, a phrase coined by early Deists was "The best of all possible worlds." Other minds may choose to believe that God acts as a combination stage manager and puppet master in controlling the events within his creation. Many of the tales found in the Jewish scriptures that Christians call The Old Testament reveal a belief in this type of deity. He is one who parts the Red Sea to save his chosen ones, then provides manna from Heaven to feed them. He causes the fortress walls to fall before them and even stops the sun in the sky for a battle to continue. It is this personal miracle-working overseer that Archibald MacLeish alludes to when he has one of his characters say, "If God is God he is not good. If God is good he is not God."[7] This is the deity, beloved by many, who simply cannot be reconciled with actual life events. I know of no one who can reconcile this loving, protective deity with the Holocaust in which millions of innocent men, women, and children were brutally slaughtered. I can neither love nor respect a deity who would choose to have children born with insurmountable handicaps that will severely limit their ability to enter into anything resembling a normal life. I cannot have any affection for a god who would choose to destroy a young family and take the lives of a young father or mother by having a drunken driver crush them with an automobile. A deity who knowingly creates or allows floods, hurricanes, tornadoes or raging fires to destroy entire villages of innocent, hard working people is not a deity I care to worship and/or obey. Whenever I hear some liturgist begin a service of worship with the phase, "God is good," and hear the congregational response, "All the time," I have to fight the urge to stand and demand: "Tell me how God is good all the time! Tell the parents here who just lost their infant child! Tell the person who just lost his job after years of faithful service! Tell the young bride who just received a telegram from the Defense Department. Explain it to the wife who just put her husband of thirty five years into an Alzheimer's unit." Instead, I sit quietly pretending to be browsing the bulletin until the entire litany has ended. If the greeting was explained on occasion to help us grasp the underlying benevolence of God in this world of random violence and mishaps, I might feel differently about it. Without a follow up however, I choose to ignore it.

The world is filled with too much random misery to attempt to explain it away by saying, "God has his reasons." Such a deity is not the one I find in the person of Jesus of Nazareth. I despair at a Church that blatantly ignores

7 *J.B.* by Archibald MacLeish. The Pulitzer Prize winning drama of 1959.

the realities of life and then claims to care for its members' everyday lives. I understand that God is with us during those bad times. I fervently believe in Romans 8:28, that "in all things God works for the good with those who love him and are called according to his purpose." My faith in this goes beyond mere belief. I *know* that God is our constant companion with whom we can celebrate our joys and triumphs, or we call upon for comfort, strength and guidance. It is the loving deity, presented and embodied in the person of Jesus of Nazareth, whose genuine nature has been lost in the muddle of theology and economic practicalities. I wish for us all to rediscover that loving God, and in rediscovering, to find ourselves in a genuinely honest and fulfilling relationship that empowers and guides our path while we tread this planet Earth.

If the liturgist were to begin the worship service by proclaiming, "God is with us!" and the congregation responded, "All the time!" and then the sequence was reversed to "All the time," and "God is with us." I would join in fervently. Then I would expect to hear messages from the pulpit that explain how this reality makes a difference – perhaps *the* difference – in our lives.

The God of Jesus is personal and present within each of us. This God we are told to call *Father* is not a magician who sets aside the laws of physics whenever it pleases Him. Rather, God has implanted within His creatures far more power than they realize. He has implanted wisdom within us, as well. Yet most of us live our lives unaware of these gifts, constantly seeking outside ourselves for guidance and power. Hopefully this book will assist the reader in finding and living comfortably with this loving deity we call by the simple, non-descriptive term *God.*

Summary

The belief that the disobedience of a single individual transformed a "very good" Creation into a Fallen one, which introduced sin and evil into it is, to me at least, unfounded. It is not a part of the Creation Story. Jesus never spoke of it. It is not a part of the Jewish faith. The fact that it has been piously echoed for centuries does not give it credence anymore than the long-held belief that the world was flat and was the center of the universe made that true.

Chapter Twelve

Sin and Evil

The Greek word we translate as "sin" actually means "to fall short" or "to miss the mark." It is an archery term that speaks of failure. When applied to the spiritual realm it implies moral/ethical failure. It was not Jesus but Paul of Tarsus who wrote of it as though it was a quality of being in its own right. "It is no longer I myself who do it, but it is sin dwelling in me." (Romans 7:17). We cannot be sure what Paul had in his mind when he wrote this. He might have been considering that aspect of his human personality that was prone to failure, or he might actually have thought of sin as a force in itself. It was more than four hundred years later that a North African bishop named Augustine decided that this "Sin" was an actual sexually transmitted disease that had originated with the Fall of Adam and Eve. He dubbed it "Original Sin," and the Church has, for some reason, ignored the teachings of Jesus Christ to adopt and advocate this doctrine. For the benefit of those who are unfamiliar with Augustine, I would say this: First, he had a brilliant mind. He also was quite insightful. His "Confessions" helped open the door to the understandings of the inner workings of the mind, struggling to make sense of its own conflicting emotions. The man also had unresolved sexual problems. An early prayer of his was, "Lord, make me chaste, but not today." He had an ongoing affair with an older mistress, and appeared to have difficulties in his relationship with his mother. Whenever she moved to where he was, he soon became ill and was forced to move for his health's sake. His brilliance offered some wonderful insights into the Christian teachings.

However, I believe adopting his theory of Original Sin was an error of gigantic proportions. There was no biblical basis for it unless one chose to ignore the first chapter of Genesis and interpret the second story of creation as actual historical truth rather than a mythological statement. I also would note that if it was considered to be historical truth then one must confront the question of where Cain's wife came from and why she was outside of Eden.

Actually, I have found the story of the Fall to be a good mythical explanation of the origin of sin within each of us. Having said this I feel the need to explain what I mean by *mythical.* The term, *myth,* has been misused by the media to mean a commonly held false belief. Actually, mythological language is used to speak of concepts that cannot be properly explained by ordinary prose. If we wish to explore myths rather fully we might begin to understand we live by myths. We accept the large stories that define our world, ourselves as people and or relationships to one another, to God and to Creation.

The parables of Jesus essentially are "mini myths." Jesus was a storyteller, not a news reporter. The storytellers of olden days were more than entertainers. They created new understandings or explained old ones through the telling of their stories. Even today, we may be profoundly moved – *awakened* – by having experienced a powerful drama. We walk away with a new understanding or resolve because we *lived the story* as it unfolded. Professional storytellers of old told tales that lasted for hours – even days and weeks. They unfolded, as some soap operas do, slowly introducing new characters and subplots, drawing their listeners more deeply into the stories. The listeners *cared* for those characters and discussed them with friends. They began to feel what the characters felt, vicariously sharing their lives. By the time the story concluded there would have been tears or profound relief or hilarious laughter, depending upon the plot. The parables we read in the Gospel accounts are highly abbreviated tales of this nature. If they were not, the Sermon on the Mount would have been over in less than fifteen minutes. There would have been no point in attending; it would not have been worth the walk. When we read of the feeding of the multitudes becoming hungry while listening to Jesus, it should give some idea of the true nature of his teaching. The Good Samaritan story was not a relating of an actual historic episode. It was a tale carefully crafted to create an understanding of a truth that transcended the social truths of the day. The same can be said of the so-called Parable of the Prodigal Son. I say "so-called," because if you read it with fresh eyes your will see that Jesus is speaking of the nature of God as a waiting, ever-forgiving Father.

Imagine how Jesus might have presented this mini-myth to his listeners. First, remember that the prevailing understanding of God was as a judge, nestled high in the sky. Like some celestial Santa Claus, he kept track of whether one was naughty or nice and dispensed punishments or rewards accordingly. Jesus introduces the Father at work in the field, hot and sweaty, busily clearing weeds away from the crop. His young son then is introduced, also hot and sweaty. He pauses from his labor, and surveys the field: everywhere he gazes he sees men and women bent over, removing the weeds, putting them in baskets on their back and moving further along the rows. He shakes his head and says to himself that this is not the life he wishes to live. He drops his small trowel, strides over to his father and announces that he wants his share of the inheritance. The father studies his young son for a moment and then agrees to allow it. Jesus then has his listeners follow the irresponsible life of the son as he wastes his inheritance . . . and himself in the process. He introduces the older son who is the model of obedience and diligence, self-righteously pouring himself more fully into the work of the farm. The other workers may admire him but they do not feel any affection for him. He is wrapped up in himself, working to increase the productivity of the farm that now will be completely his. From time to time Jesus gives a glimpse of the father absentmindedly staring down the road where he last saw his younger son disappear. He prays a silent prayer for his safety and wellbeing, then he returns to his labors. Somewhere in the course of the story, the listeners begin to understand that the father of whom Jesus is speaking is The Father of whom he speaks when he speaks of God. When the young son finally struggles home, beaten by the world, betrayed by his own foolish self-centeredness, there is a hushed moment of uncertainty in his audience. Then when Jesus tells of the father, seeing his son, dropping his trowel and racing to greet and embrace his wayward son, there is a feeling of relief and joy among them. No recriminations! No calling for remorse or apology! "My son who was lost is home again. Kill the fatted calf and let's have a party!"

Then, just when his listeners believe the story is over he introduces another theme. The father noticing that the older son is not at the party walks outside to search for him. He finds him staring at the evening sky, kicking up dirt with his feet. When he sees his father the son begins to act like a spoiled, petulant child. "I've been here working with you all the time, and what do I get?" he demands. The father places his hand lovingly on his son's shoulder and replies, "You've been with me all the time." To this, the son angrily responds, "That's what I said: What do I get?" Patiently, the father repeats himself, "You've been with me all the time." This dialogue repeats itself again and again, until even the densest of the crowd begins to understand. They want to cry out: "Don't you get it, you dummy? Your reward was being with him all the time, but you were so caught up in yourself and your self-righteousness that you missed all the joy that could have been."

I imagine Jesus then gave them a quiet nod, as if to ask, "Do you get it?" On their way home, everyone who had heard that mini-myth parable mulled over that part of the story that touched their lives; some related to the younger son; some related to the older son and began to rethink their relationship with The Father.

No prosaic explanation would have had the impact as this fictional fable laden with hidden truths. These were the stories – the myths – that unfolded new understandings that could not be expressed nearly so well in prosaic language. The Near Eastern mind of the first century easily understood the nature and purpose of mythological language. The myth of the Fall speaks of Adam being created as a simple, unselfconscious human being. However, when he and Eve ate from the fruit of knowledge they immediately became aware of – and ashamed of - their nakedness. They tried to hide from God. Adam blamed Eve; Eve blamed the serpent. Neither of them wanted to take responsibility for their actions. The result was separation: separation from God, from one another . . . and even from their true selves. The emergence of self-awareness begins the sense of the Fall within us. The spiritual, "Sometimes I feel like a motherless child - a long, long way from home," or its equivalent, often echoes deep within us. Somewhere deep within most of us the myth of The Fall resounds in our souls.

The Fall is lived out by every one of us in the process of our growing to become the fullness of the image of God. It is an essential first step to beginning the spiritual journey that will last forever. Somewhere in our second year our ego begins to form. Ego development is a crucial first step to our becoming fully human. The ego gives us boundaries that separate and distinguish us from others. A strong ego makes us firmly aware of who we are, what we value, what we believe, what we desire – in short, a strong ego allows us to clearly define who we are and who we are not. A weak ego generally causes a person to become a figment of someone else's imagination. "What do you want me to be – to do? I will become or do what you want." A strong ego, incidentally, should not be confused with a large ego. As you will soon read, a large ego is a manifestation of sin. Parents know this period of ego development as "The Terrible Twos." The child is learning to define her/himself. "No!" "Me!" "Mine!" are just a few of the words that pour forth readily from the child during this period. If parents succeed in "taming" the child, and developing a quieter, more docile child, they probably also have succeeded in weakening the strength of that child's ego (either that or developing a rebel, waiting for the opportunity). That weak ego strength will limit the child throughout his or her life. A strong sense of self and the boundaries of that self are essential to healthy development.

As ego develops the individual become more self-centered, as a matter of process. This self-centeredness is what I called the *Essence of Sin.* Egocentricity is the term used to describe the quality that causes an individual to consider and value whatever is more directly related to the person as more important than that which is less directly related. It is the core dynamic of every act we call sinful. I will illustrate: the most common expression of our egocentricity is apparent in our conversations. We listen with but half an ear. While the other person is speaking a part of us may be thinking about something else. We may be planning our response, or our mind may have wandered to something more closely related to us – and consequently more important – that we want to offer as a response. Rarely do we give the speaker enough of our attention to appreciate the full meaning to the speaker of what is being shared. If what we are hearing differs from our own belief our impulse is to dismiss the speaker as erroneous and we begin to formulate our rebuttal. We read or hear an account of a tragic accident, and upon learning the victims' names feel a sense of relief that "it is no one we know," as though the loss and suffering is no longer important simply because it does not directly affect *us*.

These are natural reactions . . . for most of us simply because most of us are quite egocentric. No matter how well we behave, no matter how caring we are, most of us still live far more within our own personal small circle of self-concern than we realize.

Every traffic violation, every driving discourtesy is caused by self-centeredness. By self-centeredness I do not necessarily mean selfishness, although it may progress to that. I simply mean that the individual is far more aware of – and concerned for – the self than for others who share the same road. Being oblivious to the needs and rights of the others, a person may turn or switch lanes without signaling (very common); ignore the speed limit because of a perceived need to rush; drink excessively and drive; talk on a cell phone in heavy traffic, or text under any condition; cut into a crowded lane at a reduced speed; race through amber or red lights at intersections or drive well beneath the posted speed limit on a two lane road or in the left-hand lane. Think about it and you will understand what I mean. These all are acts caused by our self-centeredness. The perpetrator simply is unaware or unconcerned for the others on the road. They often are perceived as obstacles; rarely as persons of worth trying to make their way, and absorbed in their own thoughts.

Every marital problem and every act of child or spousal abuse is caused by self-centeredness. It is the placing our own interests far above others with little or no genuine awareness or concern for the effect this will have on others. I repeat: we are not being guided or goaded by some satanic being. We simply are not as aware or concerned with them as with ourselves. All thieveries, all violence and all manipulation of others for personal gain obviously fall into that same category of self-centeredness.

At this point I will assume that more illustrations are needlessly redundant. Suffice it to say that the extent of our egocentricity determines the extent of the sins we commit as an act of being a human-in-process. A personal consequence of our egocentricity is a sense of isolation – of being disconnected. Like Adam and Eve we find ourselves at enmity with the earth, never or rarely feeling totally at home or totally connected with anyone . . . even ourselves.

EVIL

I simply cannot accept the idea of a second, lesser deity who resides in the "Dark Realm" trying to draw people to worship and/or follow him. This idea was introduced into Jewish thought during the reign of the Persian Empire circa 350 B.C.E. Prior to that, circa 780-750 B.C.E., in Amos 3:6 we find the prophet inquiring, "Shall evil befall a city, and YHWH not done it?" The question was rhetorical; the implied answer was, "Of course not." Once Persian dualism had become a part of the culture, the religious philosophers abandoned their pure monotheistic view of the world and began to search for links to this god of the underworld in their earlier writing. Literature majors would call these "types." The first they found was the Serpent in the Garden of Eden tale. Had the writer meant a evil deity he would have described him as such. Actually that portion was no more than an adaptation of a folk tale explanation of why snakes had no legs. A later "type" was found in the story of Job, which incidentally was not a Jewish tale. Actually it was incorporated from Mesopotamia by the Jews to raise the unanswerable question of why the righteous person suffers. In Job, Satan was not a villain. When God raved about the loyalty and devotion of his servant, Job, Satan doubted Job's sincerity and offered to test him to see if he actually was worthy of God's esteem. Some confusion arose when Greek became the dominant language of the known world and the Jewish Scriptures were translated into that language. The Greek word *perizomai* can be translated as "to test" or "to tempt." In their desire to identify Satan as a type of evil deity, they chose to make him "The Tempter." Anyone who reads the story should be aware that Satan was not tempting Job. He put Job through every terrible ordeal imaginable in an attempt to diminish his trust in God. Diablolos, or The Devil, was a Persian deity who entered Hebrew culture in the 7th century B.C.E.. Until that time there was no concept of a divine power of evil. I have read and heard every explanation of why God allows the Devil to do what he does. I stay with Ockham's Razor: "The simplest explanation is the most likely and most acceptable." There is no logical explanation for a totally good and loving deity to create a lesser deity to oppose him. We either have pure monotheism or we do not. The entire structure of the universe suggests there is but one designer and force.

So, what, then is the source of evil? The comic strip character Pogo said it well: "We have met the enemy and he is us." Scripture offers gradations on the path to evil. There are three terms people tend to think of as synonymous, but have distinctly different meanings. They are sin, stray, and trespass. I explain them as the degrees by which our humanity moves from innocence to evil. My definition of evil is this: that which intentionally harms or destroys another person – or anything of value - for its own selfish purpose.

The first step toward becoming evil is what we call *sin*. We may mean well, but as Jesus said, "The spirit is willing but the flesh is weak." (Matthew 26:41) We fall short of accepted moral/ethical standards because of our egocentricity and immaturity. Hopefully, we learn and mature along the way and stop making the same mistakes. We have powerful, primal urges and instincts that can override our logic. This was Paul's dilemma which he defined as "So I find this law at work: Although I want to do good, evil is right there with me. For in my inner being I delight in God's Law, but I see another law at work within me, waging war against the law of my mind, and making me a prisoner of the law of sin at work within me" (Romans 7:21-23). For one who had no knowledge of psychology, Paul made an astute observation of his quandary.

The next step is *to stray*. Rather than falling short of accepted standards we lose our way and our awareness of the standards. We overstep boundaries in an attempt to satisfy some need or desire. Like the lost sheep we simply wander off the proper path. However, when we stray we can find our way back. I have known individuals who strayed for lengthy times until they came to their senses and returned home. They never thought of themselves as less than good and were able to rationalize their straying. Actually, they never thought of themselves as lost, except in retrospect. Eventually, however, there was a moment of clarity, or someone reached out and helped them to find their way home.

The third step is *to trespass*. This is straying gone wild. The individual is aware that he has left the proper path and crossed into forbidden territory, but simply does not care. The attraction in the forbidden area is too strong to resist. This may take various forms. It could be that the individual has ignored the advice Paul gave to the Ephesians when he wrote, "Be angry but do not sin, and do not let the sun set on your anger." (Ephesians 4:26)

Nursed anger eventually becomes hatred. Nursed hatred can eventually consume every decent emotion and erupt into destructive action. We are aware of the mass shootings in schools and theaters by deranged individuals who had allowed themselves to become evil. There are those who have ignored the tenth Commandment and indulged themselves in coveting. It may have been lust, greed, power, or some other emotion that triggered them. Eventually that emotion consumed the better qualities within them until they believed they had to act to acquire what they desired so devoutly. Moral trespassing moves from the realm of falling short – or sin. It easily crosses into the realm of evil. Evil is that which intentionally damages or destroys for its own pleasure. Any act of sexual molestation is evil. Any act of bullying is evil. Both of these intentionally injure another human solely for the purpose of satisfying some desire in the perpetrator. They have their origin in our egocentricity, but they have stretched far beyond acceptable moral standards. The longer that person spends time in the negative realm, or the more often that person chooses to cross over to that realm – in actuality or in fantasy - the nearer that person comes to residing there. He enjoys it. He desires it. He knows it is wrong but that does not deter him. At some point, to use the terms of Sci-fi literature, the individual takes the final step. He has crossed over to the dark side and has become *evil*. With malice of forethought he will do that which is intentionally destructive to society and to individuals. His egocentricity now dominates him. Psychologists may diagnose him as a sociopath. He no longer shares concern for the needs and rights of others. Everything now is focused on *his* well-being – *his* pleasures – *his* wants. This can happen with a family member who abuses or neglects the family for himself. It may be a businessman who abuses his workers and cheats his customers. It may turn a once respectable person into a murderer or a rapist. A national leader may become a monster to his people. A Satan or Devil may serve a psychological need for some, because it is always more pleasant to reach outside of ourselves for the source of our problems. However, *Evil* is not an outside source. It is self-imposed. It is the individual, whose egocentricity has taken control, diminishing all worthy instincts and urges.

I would note that there are those persons suffering from chemical imbalances or other illnesses that may cause actions we term evil. Although the consequences may be terrible, these people are ill – not evil.

I have come to believe that our task in life is to first develop a strong ego and then to spend the remainder of our life moving from self-centeredness to God-centeredness. I use this term with the understanding that God's nature is love. To be God-centered is to have your life centered on God's agape love for all of God's Creation.

It is time to explain love as used by those who lived in the first century: The Greeks had various words that we translate as love. *Eros* speaks of romantic love and *philia* defines a form of Platonic love – a deep friendship. The term used most often in Scripture is *agape*. In my thinking, love is a poor, inadequate translation. The King James Bible uses *charity* as its translation of *agape*. In our time, charity has the connotation of a dispassionate giving of money. People hungered for a more meaningful term, so love was the term selected. I believe a better translation would be the phrase "*active, nurturing, care.*" It has nothing to do with fondness. Remember that Jesus called upon us to "love your enemies" (Matthew 5:44). Surely he did not expect us to feel affection, but he did expect us to provide for their needs, spiritual and physical. The Red Cross in combat carries out that command. Their concern is not for the uniform but for the living soul in that uniform. Medics and combat medical teams fulfill this demand, as well. The proper translation of the beloved (but mistranslated) passage from the Gospel of John is, "In this way God loved the world, in that he sent his only son that whoever believed (implies trusted) in him should not perish but have life everlasting (John 3:16). When read properly you see that it says *agape* is an action verb. The act of loving was the act of giving his son. Without a meaningful action of nurturing concern there is no love – no *agape*. A person does not become a follower of Jesus Christ by simply passively believing. *Only by actual nurturing, caring action for others does one begin to become an authentic follower.*

Since the teachings of Augustine began to dictate the thinking in the Western Church, the understanding of humanity was that we had inherited the fallen nature of our forebear, Adam. We are sinners, fallen humanity in need of redemption. Our liturgies and hymnals are filled with this designation. We are told to repent of our sins and to confess our sins. Many worship services begin with a mandatory prayer of confession. Often this is followed by a declaration of our forgiveness, but next week the ritual will be repeated.

We seem to accumulate sins in the same way that we grow our hair: it is part of our nature to do so.

Now

There is an increasing awareness of the destructiveness of this attitude toward humanity. In a way I believe the early church fathers never intended, we have slowly become spiritual masochists who cannot feel good unless we have first been made to feel bad about ourselves. I still am haunted by a discussion in a so-called liberal clergy meeting in which someone, citing Paul, claimed to be "chief among sinners." (1 Timothy 1:12-17) Another clergyperson stood and protested that he was the chief among sinners. Soon almost everyone there was vying for the chief sinner position. It was bizarre! This, frankly, was one of those moments that set me searching deeper for an understanding of where we as a church had gone wrong. Neither guilt nor shame ever were controlling factors in the home in which I was raised. Rather, we were affirmed in one another's efforts, no matter how feeble. Wrongs, and there were many, were corrected on the spot and then forgotten. Our parents never mentioned past failures. We were raised believing we were worthy and reasonably competent people. My parents never carried a grudge, and I believe I grew up assuming that if God got upset with me, He would get over it. As I read and heard the Scriptures I heard those passages in which God proclaimed his creation to be very good. When I encountered the 18th chapter in the Book of Ezekiel I almost shouted in exaltation. I felt vindicated. This spokesman for God whose visions told the exiles in Babylon that God did not reside in the Temple of Jerusalem, but traveled in his chariot so that they were not abandoned (Ezekiel 10); and told of the dead bones of Israel being renewed and restored in the valley (Ezekiel 37) also told of God's forgiving nature. In 18:21-23 he proclaims:

> *It may be that a wicked man gives up his sinful ways and keeps all my laws, doing what is just and right. That man shall live, he shall not die. None of the offenses that man has committed shall be remembered against him; he shall live because of his righteous deeds. Have I any*

desire, says the Lord God, for the death of a wicked man? Would I not rather that he mend his wicked ways and live?

Not only is guilt a destructive dynamic when used as a primary tool for obedience or conformity, I have found it to be counterproductive in changing behavior. When guilt is laid on someone the immediate felt-need is to be rid of that guilt. It is not a sudden concern for another person who may have been wronged. Guilt is not the same as remorse. A remorseful person regrets having hurt another. The victim is the primary focus. With guilt, the desire to is to be rid of a sense of worthlessness – dirtiness. A great deal of rationalization and symbolic expressions of concern tend to accompany the actions of those whose motivation is guilt. I have observed that far too many times not to recognize and understand it.

I recall being in Ann Arbor when Martin Luther King Jr. was assassinated. A citizens committee was organized to see what could be done to further the cause of human rights. There were hundreds at the initial meeting. We organized into sub-groups to brainstorm ideas. I forget how often we met, but at every meeting there were fewer of us. At a certain point I began to hear phrases like, "They really do not want our help." "There is not much we really can do." "Let's wait and see what develops, then maybe we can be of help." Eventually the committee dissipated to where there no longer were enough to continue meeting. These were good people, well-intentioned people – very bright people - but they were motivated by a vague sense of "White Guilt" and this simply was not sufficient to accomplish anything of value.

Summary

God does not say he will *forgive* the man's sins. He says the sins will be *forgotten.* I have heard Jesus proclaiming forgiveness of sins to those who did not request it. Through the words of Scripture I have heard Jesus telling an entire congregation that they were the light of the world (Matthew 5:14). Most importantly, I have listened as Jesus told about the one he called "Your heavenly Father." Finally I realized if God wants us to call him *Father*, we must be his children. *Child of God* is our proper name – not *Sinner.* When we actually believe and realize the implications of that, our lives will begin to change. Slowly, but with certainty, our lives *will* change and we will begin to live as God's children. At the core of our being we all are family. Scientists will tell you we share almost the identical DNA. Researchers have traced that DNA to common ancestors. At the spiritual level we are brothers and sisters even if we do not recognize that. Our egocentricity may try to convince us that we are different – somehow better – than others. But we are not. Yes, some cultures developed in areas that gave them an edge in the quality of their culture. Still, - to be candid – neither you nor I did anything to affect that development. We just happened to be born in the circumstances developed by many, many others. We humans really are a single, large, scattered family, differentiated by our adaptation to our environment. We have differing shades of skin and different body types. Separate cultures have developed that cause us to speak different languages, to dress differently and have different expressions of beauty in form and sound. Still, each of us hungers to be loved to be a part of a community that cares and shares. Each of us has some longing for a divine being to love us and accept us and give us a sense of peace and security. We want to believe our life has some meaning - some value. "*God was in Christ, reconciling the world to Himself, not counting our trespasses against us, but calling us to be agents of reconciliation*" (2 Corinthians 5:19) should be the mission statement of everyone who would claim to be a follower of Jesus.

Chapter Thirteen

Atonement

Reparations made for an injury or a wrong.

When I first had the doctrine of atonement explained to me in my seventh grade confirmation class, I thought it made no sense at all. "Wait! Let me get this straight," I thought. "Some guy named Adam did something God told him not to do, so God has been upset with every human being since then!" "Wow! Does He carry a grudge!" The other half made even less sense. If I understood what was said it was that God was going to stay angry until some act of atonement was made that was good enough to meet His sense of justice. The catch was that none of us imperfect humans could do that. Apparently it took God about two thousand years to figure that out, then he sent His own son, who, of course was perfect, to serve as the sacrifice. Frankly by this time (remember, I was only twelve) I wondered what sort of a God we had. This is what it looked like to my young mind:

God realized He could not be reconciled to us humans until a perfect sacrifice had been made to Him.

God realized that none of us could make that sacrifice so he sent his son to be the sacrifice.

Jesus went through the motions of dying on the cross, but he knew he would rise from the dead and be back in heaven with his Father shortly after that.

So God did not *give* his son; He only *loaned* His son. He made His son go through the agony of being beaten and then crucified just so he could let bygones be bygones and get on with being our God.

That made no sense to me then and it makes no sense now.

Perhaps it was because I had become accustomed to thinking of God as a loving Father that the explanation could not possibly rationally fit into my scheme of things. Research has shown me that there is no official doctrine of Jesus' death on the cross being an act of atonement required by God before He could be reconciled with sinful humanity. There certainly is no statement from Jesus to support that notion. Rather, it is a theory that merely evolved over time that was accepted because it filled a psychological need for many people. *I believe, however, that it also has caused as much psychological damage to some as it may have helped others.*

Actually, the original understanding of the resurrection was that Jesus of Nazareth had triumphed over Death, thereby breaking the power of Death to hold any human. Charles Wesley's Easter hymn proclaims that:

Death in vain forbids him rise. Christ has opened Paradise. [8]

This made little sense to the Hellenistic mind and new explanations began to appear as Christianity spread into the Greek world. The Eastern Church proclaimed "The Divine became human that the human might become divine" and never flirted with the idea of atonement. Those who are thoroughly indoctrinated to be sinners may not believe this.

The Temple religion was based upon sacrifices offered in atonement for sins. Matthew, the most Jewish of the four Gospel accounts, added the phrase "for the forgiveness of sins" in the account of the last supper. This satisfied the Jewish mind and those others who felt a need for punishment or retribution as a necessary part of God's justice. Unfortunately, Jesus words about offering forgiveness rather than demanding an eye for a eye, have never resonated with many who would like to think of themselves as Christians. "I'm

8 "Christ the Lord is Risen Today" Hymn #302 United Methodist hymnal

an Old Testament Christian," many proclaim with a sense of self-righteousness. "Nonsense," I say to myself. "You've missed the entire point, but want to think of yourself as a Christian, in spite of that. Without the element of mercy and forgiveness, there is no Christianity."

About a thousand years after the Resurrection, Bishop Anselm of Canterbury formulated a rather detailed theology of Atonement. It was based on the sociology of his era. A lord had the right to punish his peasants for misdeeds. He also had the right to forgive those peasants – to absolve them of any consequence for their misdeeds. However, to do so would be to risk creating a chaotic society in which there was no consequence. In order to maintain order a worthy lord never relented but always insisted upon some form of atonement for the sins. Anselm reasoned that, although God had the power and authority to bestow absolution on all of humanity for the sins of Adam, to do so would offend God's own sense of justice and need for order. Since no human could provide the purity that would meet the needs of so great a sin, God, Himself, provided the sacrifice in the form of his Son, Jesus Christ. In this understanding Jesus became less of a teacher and example and more of a sacrificial lamb. His death on the cross became more significant than his resurrection. The good news about God's unconditional love, acceptance and power to give us life eternal became more of the bad news about our sinful nature and need to be rescued. In this process we also ran into a constant contradiction: one moment we are told of God's unconditional, relentless love; the next moment we are reminded that Christ died to redeem us from our sins.

Somewhere along the way, I believe Anselm lost track of the statement God made in Isaiah 55:8, "For my thoughts are not as your thoughts, nor are your ways my ways, says the Lord." It is this human necessity of creating God in our image that has been the cause of distorting our faith to the point where it would not be recognized today by Jesus of Nazareth. I believe it is the underlying cause of every heresy, every misconception and every distortion of thought the Church has suffered over the centuries. The Creator of this extraordinary universe does not think as we mere humans think. I also believe that God's sense of justice more nearly resembles what Jesus proclaimed by his life and actions, than what we humans practice. While I do not believe I can begin to define the purpose of God's creation of humanity I fervently believe God did not create us with the thought of punishing us for being what he has made us to be.

The God I find revealed in Jesus Christ has no need for atonement. Jesus forgave sins even before people asked him to do so (Mark 2:5). When asked about how many times we should forgive, Jesus answered, "seventy times seven" (Matthew18:22). Beyond that, I always thought it strange that even though Jesus paid the price for our sins on the cross, we have to confess those sins every week and then receive forgiveness for them. I hear people say and sing words about "all of my sins upon that cross." I realize they are making a powerfully emotional statement about feeling free of the dirt and grime they still feel is packed up around their soul. A part of them feels clean, but there is some underlying residue of sinfulness that continues to sting, and I sense a soul still suffering unnecessarily.

For me, the doctrine of Atonement creates and nurtures the very illness it claims to heal. I recall a study made back in the 1960's in which a group of researchers became aware that the elderly Christians in nursing homes seem to be more afraid of dying than those who claimed no religious faith. Upon further investigation they realized that this was because of a fear of the final judgment. No matter how many times they had received words of forgiveness, deep within themselves they thought they had done things that not even God could forgive. One of the fears that plagued Martin Luther was his awareness that he probably had not confessed every sin he had committed, and therefore had unforgiven sins on his account book.

In my retirement I once was called upon to fill in at the last minute for a friend who had become ill. The text for his sermon included Proverbs 23:13-14:

> *Do not withhold discipline from a boy; take a stick to him and save him from death.*
>
> *If you take the stick to him yourself you will preserve him from the jaws of death.*

I took issue with that phrase and stated, "whoever wrote that was wrong." My preacher friend thanked me for filling in but told me he had received a few phone calls on the following Monday, expressing some concern for the substitute preacher's biblical faith. I thought we were far past the Calvinistic admonition to "beat the devil out of our children" (yes, that is the origin and meaning of the term). It seems, however, that many who would think of ourselves as good Christians, are more prone to follow past training or base impulses than to give credence to the words of one we purportedly call "Lord."

Guilt and punishment are not worthy Christian doctrines. Our God is a redemptive, loving God! Belief of demands for Atonement before God could forgive does not exalt God's righteousness. No matter how well intentioned, it demeans Him.

In his parable called The Prodigal Son, Jesus describes a father whose love is unconditional. The father does not require an apology or any form of repayment or restitution from his returning son. The son does not return because he regrets leaving his father, nor because he regrets what he did to him. He returns home because, as Robert Frost states so simply in his poem, "The Death of the Hired Man": "*Home is the place that when you have to go there, they have to take you in.*" The father embraces him and celebrates his return. If God is, indeed, this loving Father Jesus proclaimed him to be, then God is far more interested in our growing into His likeness than in punishing us. There still is far too much child abuse in our society today. We have come to recognize how destructive this is and now have laws and agencies to prevent it. The biblical "Spare the rod and spoil the child" no longer serves as justification in a court of law.

For those persons who cannot believe they could be forgiven with no strings attached, atonement might serve as a starting place for their spiritual journey in Christ. However, the Church needs to get beyond that thinking and quickly move any spiritual pilgrim from that understanding of God.

There is no now – no future – for this outdated and destructive doctrine in the new paradigm church. This misconception must be replaced by a more worthy, more constructive and healing explanation of Jesus' death on the cross.

I would offer this alternative to atonement: Christians are generally in agreement that God's nature is Love. We use the Greek term *agape* to define that love, and incorporate the idea of active nurturing. If God's nature actually is *Lover*, then it seems only logical that God requires something or someone to love. The first time I read James W. Johnson's *God's Trombones*[9] I was drawn to the opening statement in his Creation account: "God said, 'I'm lonely' I think I will make me a world.'" Any other reason strikes me as a deity passing the time by playing solitaire. From there, I reason that God created humanity for companionship. We were not created to be servants, but partners (God had no need for servants). We were not created just to give glory, thanks and praise to God (God has no ego needs). We may have the need to praise and express our gratitude to God, but our loving Father has no need for these expressions.

The idea that our God would require some form of retribution in order to forgive the actions of some long-ago ancestor not only is insulting to God, but it is in direct contradiction of the statements made by Ezekiel. I have mentioned the 18th chapter of Ezekiel in which he carefully develops his thesis that God does not judge any person by what a forebear did. He began the chapter with this statement:

> *These were the words of the Lord to me: What do you all mean by repeating this proverb in the land of Israel:*
>
> *"The fathers have eaten sour grapes, and the*
> *children's teeth are set on edge?"*

9 Johnson, James, *God's Trombones*, London: Penguin Books, 1927

He concluded it with this:

> *It is the soul that sins, and no other, that shall die; a son shall not share his father's guilt, nor a father his son's.*

Forgiveness by God has no part in our redemption. God does not hold grudges. Jesus acted this out by pronouncing forgiveness easily and readily. He knew people perceived God as a judge, so they felt the fear and burden of their sins. Jesus spoke words of forgiveness to set people free of this unnecessary burden. Then he told them to set it right with the person who had been wronged (Matthew 5:23-24).

Augustine may have been a powerful thinker and persuasive writer, but it is obvious that he either never read Ezekiel or he chose to ignore it. So, we are faced with a dilemma: either we ignore what authoritative Scripture says – or we ignore Augustine and those who parrot his teachings. Let's take a closer look at this thing we call forgiveness before we decide.

The traditional expression of our faith requires us to confess our sins of commission and omission in order to receive God's forgiveness. "The things we have done and the things we have left undone," just about covers it. In spite of regular confessions, however, many of us are walking closets of guilt. "If people really knew who I was . . ." is a silent chant that softly plays in our minds. Guilt is somewhere at the core of our faith. It runs through our hymnals, and is the foundation of our celebration of the Lord's Supper. I sometimes refer to the medieval Church as "An Ecclesiastical Car Wash." Just as many of us regularly drive through a car wash to rinse away the superficial dirt, so the medieval Church required people to regularly confess and be forgiven of their surface sins, while neglecting to deal with the more deep-seated feelings of guilt.

Christians spend much of their time and energy dealing with the issue of forgiveness. I believe this is needless. God's forgiveness only is necessary if God judges us, and if there is some final moment of judgment that determines our future. I believe Jesus' task was to transform our image of a judging deity into the image of a loving parent. If we actually accept Jesus' understanding of God as a loving parent who will accept a wayward child's return without hesitation or condition, then it follows that we stop thinking in terms of reward and punishment by our God. Apparently far too many people have not experienced parents who love unconditionally, so the idea simply does not resonate within them. It is beyond their grasp, so they must temper that image to fit their own experience. Martin Luther could not say the "Our Father," because his own experience of a father was an unhappy one. As a consequence, the issue of forgiveness disturbed him throughout his life.

This idea of a loving, accepting Father God is crucial to freeing ourselves from the grips of the traditional Christianity that has dominated our culture for centuries. I started a new church in Ann Arbor in 1967. For the first five or six months I did not serve communion. Finally, a member of the church inquired, "Dick, don't Methodists serve communion?" I admitted that I had intentionally overlooked this sacrament because I wanted to find a positive liturgy by which to celebrate it. I realized that everything we did set precedence for us. Fortunately I went to a nationwide convocation on worship where there were some people who were far ahead of me in my thinking. There were liturgies that properly celebrated the Eucharist as a joyful expression of thanksgiving for God's gift of Jesus Christ. When I returned home I printed copies of the new liturgy, and asked the congregation to compare the new with the unused traditional. As part of the morning's sermon we discussed it. One bright, young lady, Cindy Dean, remarked, "The old one has built-in failure." I sensed Cindy was onto something important, so I encouraged her to explain. "The old says we have failed to be obedient and have not cared for those in need," she said. "Then it asks God to make us more obedient." She paused, and then proceeded. "However," she said with a sense of exasperation, "we know when we return for communion next month we are going to say we failed one more time." "That's it!" I thought. Intuitively I had known that prayer was destructive. I had felt it in my bones, but it took someone who had never seen that prayer before to look at it with fresh eyes and spot the problem.

One of the great theologians of the last century was Paul Tillich. A much-read sermon of his during the middle years of that century was "You are Accepted." It spoke to a deep hunger within the hearts of almost all of us. Somehow, unfortunately, that message was drowned out by the likes of a Billy Graham and his ilk, who insisted upon proclaiming the bad news of our sinful nature as a preface to the Good News of God's unconditional love. We were told to confess our sins in order to receive forgiveness.

Let's think of God as a loving parent who's desire for us is that we grow to become companions together in a family grounded in loving concern and respect for one another. I believe I was fortunate enough to have been raised in a family of that nature. I still recall a time – back when I was eleven years of age – when I really messed up. Some boys from the block behind our house had sneaked into our yard and destroyed the clubhouse we had carefully constructed from remnants we had garnered from various locales. I knew who it was: Tom Sullivan! I saw it in his response when we discovered the damage. Tom lived on the other side of the alley that divided our lots. He had watched us construct the clubhouse and had made derisive comments while we did so.

I deeply – devotedly – desired revenge.

About a week later, I observed Tom and his father constructing something out of bricks in their backyard. I assumed (incorrectly) that his father was assisting Tom in making something for Tom. That night, I and one of the club members sneaked into Tom's backyard and tore down, brick by brick, what Tom had built. I did notice that the bricks seemed sticky, but I never considered the reason. I was getting my revenge. That was all I wanted. The next day, Mr. Sullivan called all the neighborhood boys into the alley behind his house and questioned them as to who destroyed his barbeque pit. He did not question me directly, so I stood quietly watching as he spoke to each of the older boys, including my brother, George.

The Inquisition continued for days. The culprit who destroyed Mr. Sullivan's barbeque pit became the main subject of speculation in the neighborhood. My brother, who acted a bit guilty since he knew I was that culprit, was questioned again by my mother. I breathed a sigh of relief that the questioning stopped with him. We had an understanding in our house that we never were to lie to our parents. They would support us if we had done something wrong, but we were not to lie to them. Then – one evening, my mother, sensing George was involved, questioned George again. This time, however, my father watched me as she spoke. "Did you ask Dick?" he asked.

My heart sank. My mother replied that she had not. "Ask him," my dad ordered, staring directly at me. I admitted I had done the deed. Mother nearly collapsed in disbelief (I had an innocent appearing face).

Neither of my parents considered that I should apologize to them, or their needing to forgive me. I was marched over to the Sullivan house. My parents stood protectively at a distance while I rang the doorbell and confessed to Mr. Sullivan. Fortunately, Mr. Sullivan was a kindly man. He understood what I was trying to explain through my tears and stammering. My allowance was suspended until it had paid for the cement. I cleaned the damaged bricks and helped Mr. Sullivan rebuild the barbeque pit. Mr. Sullivan and I became friends. Even Tom (he helped) and I became friendlier. Eventually I restored my reputation in the neighborhood, and life moved on.

My point is that my parents did not need to forgive me, nor did I need their forgiveness. I had not wronged them. I had wronged Mr. Sullivan. My parents' only interest was that I correct my mistake as well as possible, learn my lesson and move on. If that is how loving parents act, why do we believe a loving God acts differently? Alcoholics Anonymous understands that. Admit your mistake and then set it right with those you offended. Confessing to God and then going on with your life as though the issue was settled is a cop out! All the while, my parents continued to love me and accept me for who I was at that time. Their participation was to make me understand what I had done, to set it right, learn my lesson and then get on with my life – a bit more wisely, they hoped.

So if God is not a judge who records when we have been naughty or nice in order to reward or punish us, why do we need His forgiveness? As a parent I have observed my daughters as they went through the various stages of maturing. There were moments when I knew their behavior was not what I liked, but when I thought the consequences would not permanently damage them I usually waited, held my breath and prayed. There never was a moment when I did not love or accept them for who they were at that moment. My greater concern always was with what kind of person they were becoming.

I believe I learned that from both my earthly parents and my loving Father God.

For me, the purpose of the church should not focus on the little sins of commission and omission. Rather the Church should assist its people in directing their lives to deal with the root cause of sin: *Egocentricity* and the more troublesome issue of *Ontological Anxiety* and *Ontological Guilt*. The egocentricity has been covered in the chapter on Sin. The other two are basic to our development as Children of God. *Ontological* refers to the process of *being* and *becoming*. Sometime around the age of 28-30 most of us encounter the first taste of *Ontological Anxiety*. We have followed the blueprint of our society, completing our education, securing a job and finding a mate – or deciding not to do that. We find ourselves asking, "Is that all there is?" Somewhere within us there is a deep rumbling wondering what our life is supposed to mean. Perhaps we sense that we are supposed to do more than merely mature and repopulate the earth while waiting for a comfortable retirement. For many of us this moves us into our first "mid-life crisis." We may switch careers (I made the decision to enter the ministry). We may take a up a new hobby, purchase a sports car, have an affair. Divorce often is a choice, when people believe (perhaps properly) their marriage was a mistake. The Church should and could help people to prepare for and move through this stage in a manner that is productive and worthy. The next critical stage is around age 40-42. If the first stage was not recognized and dealt with properly, this may come with much greater force. This stage is a prime time for marital problems to surface. Divorces and affairs are more epidemic.

Through its regular preaching and educational programs, any congregation could be of assistance to its members, to stabilize and direct individuals and families. An ongoing theme should be, "God is calling you to become more than you now are." Individual classes could be made aware of those stages and utilize their class time and social times to address that.

Ontological Guilt is another issue. It creeps into our lives when we believe that it is too late for us to change and become what God has called us to become. We all have heard that poignant complaint: "I finally reached the highest rung on the ladder only to discover it was leaning against the wrong wall." There are some people, of course, who cannot be helped at this stage. They have slipped into a state of guilt and despair and will refuse to leave it. They have given up and are only waiting to die. Others, however, can and may respond to new opportunities to become a bit more than they are. It is difficult to alter a life-style that has been a pattern for decades. In these instances, my own approach is to serve more as a spiritual hospice than rehabilitation center.

Summary

Confession and forgiveness is akin to placing a Band-Aid on an infected wound. The real issues run deeper and can be addressed by congregations willing to do so.

At one level I believe Jesus never explained the reason for his death for the same reason that he taught in parables. They are open to interpretation by different people in different circumstances and different times in their lives. Some people are so consumed by feeling of guilt that the fact that Jesus "took all my sins away" may have a powerful cathartic value. I believe they eventually need to grow beyond that to gain spiritual maturity and freedom. However, that may be as far as they can travel in this lifetime.

Utilizing Ockham's Razor, however, I would suggest that the purpose of Jesus' death is this: had Jesus not died a very public and certain death, his resurrection would have meant little. Also, his willingness to die demonstrated his conviction that his teachings were true. Had he died of an illness and then reappeared in public a few days later, most would assume he merely had recovered. A very public and certain death was required. Mark's very brief ending of his account supports that theory. He does not speak of any post resurrection sightings. He does not have to. Remember that Mark's account was the memoirs of his uncle, Simon Peter. Peter began his preaching immediately after the resurrection, and the general public knew of the resurrection. Later, the other Gospel writers had to include the sightings because time had passed, the message had spread, and there were many who had no certain witnesses of that event.

Jesus' death remains open to personal interpretation. No council ever set forth one official doctrine. For some, the belief that Christ's death washed their sins and guilt away, may be helpful as they are in the early stages of their journey. However, I believe it a destructive belief for many and should not be thrust upon them. I also believe that those who begin with a belief in Christ's atoning sacrifice should eventually abandon that and replace it with a more positive belief that affirms their essential goodness.

I believe Jesus died on the cross as part of the evidence of God's power to overcome the death of his children, and to point them to a longer view of their existence than mere life-on-earth. In other words, Jesus died and rose to prepare us for Eternity as part of God's family. He never suggested that God was upset with us because of Adam's actions. Jesus' message did not suggest reconciliation, but loving obedience. We are God's beloved children. Yes, we fall short at times. I believe we disappoint Him, but our loving Father does not disown or abandon us because of this.

This, of course, is my personal interpretation of Jesus' death on the cross. Each of us must work out our own.

Chapter Fourteen

Grace

Grace, as it is used in Scripture is an unmerited action of God's on behalf of humanity. As it is used in preaching, I think of it as a "weasel word." It is one of those wonderfully ill-defined terms that many preachers employ to move their listeners through a poorly understood idea. "But God's grace will see you through." "There but for the grace of God go I." "We can always rely on God's grace in times of crisis." When I hear grace used in these ways I invariably realize that I need to know what this grace looks like and feels like. I have to know if it is real and how it actually operates in my life.

I learned an important lesson about grace early in my ministry. It was at the University of Michigan hospital where I was doing an internship as a hospital chaplain. My supervisor questioned me about my feelings towards the indigent patients I was serving on the tuberculosis ward. I gave the automatic pious response we Christians have been taught, with no real thought of what it meant: "I realize that there but for the grace of God, go I." My supervisor never blinked. He leaned forward and asked, "Dick, can you take out the phrase, 'but for the grace of God?'" For a moment I just sat quietly, trying to process what he was asking. He decided to help me by rephrasing his question: "Dick, can you just say, 'There go I?' The grace of God has nothing to do with it." Before I could respond, he added: "Why do you believe you are so special as to receive God's grace while those men in the ward do not?" I did not say a word. I just sat quietly processing what my supervisor had asked. I felt something within me shifting. Some foundational belief I had unconsciously held since a child was slipping from under my feet. I did not utter a word, but my mind was responding: "Oh my God, you are right! You are so right!" My supervisor seemed to understand what was happening within me, so he gently added, "We all like to believe we are somehow special . . . and we all are . . . in some way. But – then – we are not at all special. We are just one more beloved child of God." After a long, silent pause . . . I nodded agreement.

I was simultaneously deflated and elated by this new understanding that had been thrust on me.

I just have been fortunate to be born in the right place to the right parents – at the right time. Pure random chance! Oh yes, I have been fortunate enough to have been given certain physical and intellectual gifts – not spectacular but adequate - to allow me to find an attractive, competent mate and get a decent job. Work ethics were inherited by osmosis and circumstances outside my control. Given a different set of conditions I might well have been one of those indigent patients in the ward. When that supervisor took away my special grace with his simple question he threw me off of my lofty pillar- right into the streets. I would like to say I never looked at an unfortunate person the same way again, but that would not be true. Carl Jung said the mind is the logos part of our being. It grasps new ideas quickly. However, he cautioned, the soul is the agricultural portion that heals and grows very slowly. I am further along in my struggle to be more fully human, but I am not there yet. Whenever I speak of any step taken in my journey, I can cite Paul's letter to the Philippians: "Not that I have already obtained this or am already perfect, but I press on to make it my own, because Jesus Christ has made me his own." (Philippians 3:12)

Grace is usually defined as "the unmerited assistance given humans for their regeneration or sanctification." The biblical definition has evolved differently over time to mean "the love and mercy shown to us by God not because of any merit on our part." I tend to think of grace as an underlying quality of creation that moves things to completion and fullness. Romans 8:28 expresses this for me: "For we know that in all things God works for the good with those who love him and are called according to his purpose."

I do not believe "those who love God" are confined to individuals who go to churches and sing hymns of praise. In fact I do not believe all of those who do that are among "those who love God." God is not contained in a name. There are many godly people who may believe they do not believe in God simply because they reject the deity they see proclaimed by many who claim to be religious. To love God is to genuinely love and embrace those qualities we attribute to God as proclaimed and seen in Jesus of Nazareth. Those persons who actually seek justice, practice compassion, treat others with respect and contribute, as they are able, to the goodness in this world are those who actually are the persons I think of as "loving God" regardless of what, if any, claim they make with their lips. In 1 John 4:20, the writer says, "Whoever claims to love God, yet hates his neighbor or sister is a liar. For whoever does not love their brother or sister whom they have seen, cannot love God whom they have not seen." The writer's word for love was *agape,* which requires genuine caring action to be real.

I have been haunted for decades by a simple sociological study I read back in the early 60's. A study was made of some primitive South Pacific tribes. As part of the study, the people were asked to identify those persons they considered to be wealthy. When the ones named were visited, the researchers could find little difference in their possessions from the average villager. Further research revealed that those considered "wealthy" were very competent farmers with good soil. At the conclusion of the harvest season the "wealthy ones" took what they believed they needed for comfortable survival during the next growing season. Then they brought the surplus to the village center. When all the surplus food had been delivered, those who had not faired well with their crops were invited to take what they believed was required for them to survive until the next harvest. Before the day ended everyone in the village had food security. The "wealthy ones" were esteemed and their words carried extra weight in village matters. That was the extent of their wealth. Whatever ego needs they had were met. No one in the village had to suffer humiliation or hunger.

What has haunted me, of course, is the simple fact that none – not one – of the villagers was Christian. What I had vicariously witnessed was a far greater expression of communal *agape* than I have experienced in any Christian gathering. We who call ourselves Christian have had a wonderful model of living in godly love with one another. However, far too often we shame the name of Jesus by our selfish - even hateful – lack of care for those in need all around us. We like to believe that we are a Christian nation, yet we have the greatest extreme between the ultra wealthy and those who struggle daily to find sufficient food to eat. Some of those wealthy may give a pittance to charities, but any belief that they are followers of Jesus is self-deception. It is my experience that many who are outside the church or even have rejected the church may, in actuality, be more Christ-like than many who wear the cross lapel pins.

That spark of divine spirit resides in every human being – every child of an all-loving deity. It may awaken and burst forth in active care for others, or it may hibernate within us – no matter our claims to the contrary – until we have taken our final breath . . . having wasted the time given us.

Given that, I interpret Romans 8:28 to mean that those who work to make this world a kinder, safer place are in touch with an underlying quality of being that moves people and activities toward fulfillment. If they get off track and things are not working out, they step back, take a fresh look and try a different approach to the issue. Their drive to make things better keeps them trying. The end result is not necessarily a happy ending, but any situation can be made better because of their efforts – coupled with this underlying grace. "Works for the good" does not mean "everything turns out for the best," as too many naïve believers wish to think.

The great hymn, "Amazing Grace" expresses the manner in which this unseen, unfelt grace operates, when you know the story of its author. If ever a soul was lost it was John Newton. Briefly, he became a captain of a slave trading ship. He also had renounced any form of religion. One night during a terrible storm he cried out, "Lord have mercy on me," and realized there still was some spark of belief within him. He drew from that and began to regain the faith of his childhood. An illness caused him to abandon the life of a sailor. He found himself pursuing the study of this Christian faith. He married a lady who had never ceased praying for him and became a clergyman. Nothing on this journey seemed extraordinary. Yet, in reflection John called it "grace" and wrote the words of this beloved hymn. [10]

10 Turner, Steve, *Amazing Grace*, New York: Harper Collins, New York, 2002

Summary

We live in a mystery – one that we shall never fully comprehend. Yet I believe this mystery "in which we live and move and have our being" (Acts 17:28) can properly be named "God." I have heard the term coincidence defined as "God's desire to remain anonymous." Grace, to me, is the underlying benevolence in existence that moves people and events toward worthy fulfillment of their potential. It is the basis for Paul's proclamation in Romans 8:28, *"For we know that in all things God works for the good with those who love him and are called according to his purpose."*

Chapter Fifteen

Prayer

Prayer is the lifeblood of our relationship with the Divine presence we call God. It is the difference between being alongside someone and being *with* that someone. Prayer is the pathway for living in the presence of God our Father.

At seminary we were given a model for prayer: adoration, confession, thanksgiving and supplication. For some time I attempted to follow that pattern even though it seemed artificial. Eventually, however, I simply abandoned it as being just one more man-made obstacle blocking a genuine relationship with our Heavenly Father. When Paul told the Thessalonians to pray without ceasing (1 Thessalonians 5:17) he certainly did not have that structure in mind. I believe it was his way of telling them to constantly be aware of the presence of God in their lives. When Jesus was asked by his disciples to teach them how to pray, the model he offered was not the one I was taught at seminary (Luke 11:1-4).

There is no fixed pattern for conversation. Why then does anyone actually believe there must be some inflexible system for conversing with God? Frankly, I have come to believe that structured prayers are not for actual communion with God but for public consumption. It makes sure we cover all the bases. I do have one basic rule I follow when engaging in intimate conversation with God: I pause and present myself to Him and wait until I sense His Presence within me. Somewhere along the path of being married to Diane I learned not to enter the house and begin talking, as though she had been waiting all day just to hear my voice. On my better days I first present myself to her and begin to sense her as a presence in my life. So it is in prayer. I cannot pray on demand simply be closing my eyes and tossing words into empty space. I wrote these words for Diane many years ago. Somewhere along the line I realized they were the key for me to meaningful prayer:

> *Touch me before you speak. Let us measure and narrow the distance that separates us from one another. Then, when we do speak, we will need fewer words to understand one another.*

This pausing is my one and only rule for communicating with the divine Presence we call Father. I have a few personal models I *do* follow, however: I talk things over with God. As with Tevyev in *Fiddler on the Roof*, I often have a running conversation with God about what is happening in my world and my life. Unlike Tevyev, I wait for God to respond. Many times I sense his response as, "Get off of it, Dick." "Think deeper before you complain." Then God invites me to press further for understanding, always reminding me that I am the only person over whom I can exercise control. Often God allows me to understand the issue more clearly and I find Romans 8:28 kicking in.[11] I am not sure how it works, but I have learned that my life usually works better after I have had these talks with the One who knows me better than I know myself.

When I am concerned for a person or a situation I do not pray what people call the prayer of intercession. For me, this is unnecessary. Although I often tell people I am praying for them, my first step is to settle myself in quiet meditation. Then I begin to focus upon the individual in need, or the known players in the situation for which I have concern. Next I channel spiritual energy toward that person or persons. Many who read this will think I have lost some contact with reality or been struck with a bad case of megalomania. However, some will quietly nod and keep reading. It took me years of searching and struggling to finally arrive at some understanding of intercessory prayer that my mind could accept and practice with vigor and integrity.

---

11 *We know that in all things God works for the good with those who love him and are called according to his purpose.*

I have never been comfortable with the idea of making a special request to a deity who, as Jesus said, "knows all your needs." (Matthew 6:8) Those who do so will live with the unanswerable question of why God seems to answer some requests, but ignores or denies others. I have heard a plethora of futile sermons in which some well-intentioned preacher attempts to explain this (I undoubtedly was one of those preachers in my younger days). We humans have an insatiable hunger to find meaning and purpose in our lives, so there will always be those who give it a try. I eventually realized that my premise was wrong. I assumed that it was God who decided whether or not to answer a prayer and bestow whatever grace the person requested. With that premise there could never be a satisfactory answer. "God has His reasons," made no more sense to me than, "Because I'm your mother," for why I should or should not have done a certain thing.

Even though we like to believe we are special, God does not play favorites. I believe God equips us with more resources to heal ourselves, withstand adversity, affect life situations, redirect our lives, influence others, and even rise from the ashes than we dare to imagine. We are essentially spiritual creatures living in a universe in which our Creator/Sustainer is *everywhere.* We are immersed in Spirit. Every part of our being is a bundle of condensed energy. Countless billions of molecules and atoms are whirling within us at amazing speeds – containing amazing energy. We emit this energy every moment of our lives.

I believe most of us have had the experience of sitting in some public place and suddenly turning around or looking up to see some stranger staring at us. It well may be that this stranger was staring because she believed she knew us. Whatever the reason, we sensed that "presence" and responded to it. Sometimes we may have thought we were alone in a room and gradually became aware of another presence in that room. Before humans developed languages they were more sensitive to reading another's thoughts and sensing another's presence. Many married couples or long-term close friends seem to sense what the other is thinking or doing. They walk into the house and immediately sense their partner is not there. Some form of energy is what causes those events, and some of those experiences are created by focused energy. It is this energy that I channel when I pray.

The scene in Mark 9:14-29 served to open the door for me to realize the power that is overlooked in every prayer formula I have read. Jesus has come from the Mount of Transfiguration to join his disciples. He learns that they have failed to drive a demon from a child who appears to have the symptoms we now would call epilepsy. The father asks Jesus if he could cure his son. Jesus responds that anything is possible to the one who believes. The father then offers these famous words: "I believe. Help my unbelief." Jesus proceeded to cast out the demon. When his disciples asked why they could not drive the demon out, Jesus responded, "This kind can come out only by prayer." I noticed that there was not even a suggestion that Jesus had prayed for the child to be free of the demon. He had simply commanded the demon to be gone, and the child was cured.

I do not want to open a discussion on the reality of demons. People operate within the framework of their paradigm. Jerome Frank presented that issue quite well in his book, *Persuasion and Healing.*[12] Rather I want to examine Jesus' explanation to his disciples. I believe Jesus' statement, "You unbelieving generation," was directed as an admonishment to his disciples. There was no reason to blame the others who knew nothing of him. Jesus made a practice of early morning solitary prayer. (Mark 1:35) This was his special time with the Father. It was the time when he affirmed the ties, and recharged himself. All energy within the universe is derived from the One we have learned to call Father. He drew deeply from this energy. It was what empowered him, renewed his soul and directed his path.

As with every other attribute we share in common, this spiritual energy and the ability to channel it – or receive it - are not shared in identical degrees. Yet all of us, to some degree, have those attributes. It is this *recharging prayer* that, for me at least, is the necessary time of prayer by which we begin our day. This is the one I fear we tend to overlook. Without it, we are trying to go it alone.

I believe there is power in this type of prayer. I also believe that there is strength in numbers. Years ago I planned to give a midweek evening service homily which used the story of the crippled man being lowered through a roof to be healed by Jesus. (Mark 2:1-10) I had intended to ask the worshipers to hold some person whom they knew in prayer through the evening. Just as

---

12 Frank, Jerome, *Persuasion and Healing: a comparative study of psychotherapy*, Baltimore: The John Hopkins University Press, 1961

the service was about to start I was informed that a young man in the congregation had been sent to the ER with suspect meningitis, and might not live through the night. I changed my plan and requested that everyone hold this young man in prayer. Later I learned that the young man, who actually had meningitis, was declared well and sent home two days later. Coincidence? Perhaps. I have heard coincidence defined as "God's desire to remain anonymous." This is but one example of many I have encountered over fifty years of ministry. People do not have to be gathered together for multiple prayers to be effective.

Summary

Prayer is far more than the models usually offered. Prayer is a lifestyle. It is living in the awareness of God's continuing presence in our lives. Sometimes prayer is a matter of channeling your spiritual energy, directing it to the person or situation of concern.

If your present prayer model seems to work for you, stay with it. I have no desire to change anyone's way of relating to the Divine. My models are offered for those who are not satisfied with what they presently have.

Chapter Sixteen

Salvation

When I encounter some pious Christian who asks me if I've been saved, I have of a few standard responses I offer, depending on my mood at the time:

1. "I've been saved and lost so many times I honestly cannot tell you which I am at the moment."

2. "Of course. (This requires a pious look) It was on a hill outside of Jerusalem nearly two thousand years ago."

I realize these people are not so much interested in knowing if I have been saved, as in letting me know that *they* have been saved. I have learned that either response precludes further discussion. However, if I suspect that the person actually desires a rational discussion I answer honestly, "I do not use that term anymore." Many years ago I presided at a funeral for a friend who had been in my congregation many years earlier. I observed that the mixture of mourners was consistent with my friend's life-style. There were conservatives, moderates, liberals, and a few who had little if any faith. As I began my remarks I felt compelled to say, "In the seven years I served as Ron's pastor we never spoke of his being saved or not." I noticed an aroused sense of interest in all who were there. I continued with, "Because it never once occurred to either Ron or me that the God we both served so lovingly and joyfully was someone from whom we needed to be saved." The reaction startled me:

Everyone there was nodding in agreement.

As I reflected upon that I wondered whether some of them merely recognized the truth of that when I said it, or if they always felt that way, but appeared to accept their church's theology in order for themselves to be accepted. Early in my ministry I thought of myself as a teacher who gave people information that allowed them to become freer and more in touch with the depth and power of their faith. Later, however, I began to understand that I also was a *permission giver.* Time and time again, after my presentation, I will have one or more persons approach me and say, "I have always thought that way." Because I was ordained, had the doctoral credentials and stated my beliefs publicly, many long-term traditional Christians felt comfortable coming out of their "heretical closets."

I attended my church's confirmation class when I was twelve years of age. The teacher, a well-intentioned loving person, told us that the secret to being saved was to believe Jesus was raised from the dead, and be able to say he was God's Christ. Many years later I realized that she was merely expressing what Paul had written in Romans 10:9:

> *If you confess with your mouth that Jesus is Lord and believe in your heart that God raised him from the dead, you will be saved.*

I remember thinking that if that really was all there was to it, God could have worked it out better (I was only twelve and had not yet developed proper piety in my thinking). "All God would have to do," I thought, "was to have Jesus waiting at the place where the newly dead assembled. He then could give them the option of believing and confessing and going to heaven, or denying and going to hell." I remember thinking it would be a lot more efficient and there probably would be a 100% success rate. I know that sounds foolish, but I was twelve at the time and it seemed to make sense. As I continued to ponder the idea, I realized there had to be more to it than that. Paul kept writing to tell people what they should or should not be doing. Eventually I came to the conclusion that belief was just the first step.

I have talked with far too many former church members who have told me they left the church because of the outdated teachings they find unbelievable and meaningless. I also have been long-haunted by a statement made by a brilliant professor during an almost raucous discussion: "Why is it that in this classroom all of you are so honest – and then when you climb into your pulpits on a Sunday you lie like hell." I was angered by this, so I stood up and shouted back, "I do not do that!" The professor looked at me for a long moment then replied, "No, you probably do not." Then he waved his hand generally around the room and said, "But all of the rest of them do." There was silence, but not one of the other students protested. I was aghast! Too many clergy have allowed themselves to be intimidated by a few older members who have deep pockets and an inflexible allegiance to "that old time religion."

If belief is a primary step in a genuine spiritual journey then the belief must either be a belief in a reality or a false idea. So I ask how in the world anyone with integrity can profess something not believed as a means of guiding others? Talk about false prophets – or perhaps it should be "False Profits!" There are those who lie and mislead their congregations for personal gain. They preach a false gospel simply because there are people who will pay well to hear it so they can justify their selfishness and prejudices. That is despicable. There are far more, however, who withhold some of the truths they learned in seminary out of fear. Unfortunately we have many good church members who refuse to let go of cherished beliefs, even though they are false. They intimidate their pastors and place unseen barriers against new members by insisting on clinging to a dead past. Changing the theological thinking of a congregation is not an easy task. However, I believe faithful pastors can begin to make significant changes in the underlying preaching, prayers and hymns that can move their congregations into the new and empowering paradigm. The first step is to draw forth the positive message about the nature of humanity from Scripture. Tell them time and time again that they are the children of God, made in God's own image and were made live by God's spirit breathed into them. Remind them they are the light of the world. Remove the dreadful prayer of confession from the communion ritual that has built-in failure. Use the hymns that call forth the best in them. Preach sermons that offer hope and affirm their faith. Preach sermons that speak to the needs of society and the personal struggles of your congregation. Preach from reality and not website illustrations. If you need to use the old paradigm for interpretation of Scripture, so be it. Then if a congregation refuses to listen to reasoned, scripturally supported preaching and teaching, but insists upon hearing only the messages they wish to hear, it is best to leave them to their own darkness of soul. Those I know who have done that have maintained their integrity and found congregations who desired to be led by them. Here I draw from Matthew 7:6:

> *Do not give what is holy to the dogs, and do not throw your pearls before swine, or they will trample them under their feet and turn and tear you to pieces.*

Now

Most active Christians I know do not seem to worry about having been "saved." Their focus is more on their present lives and relationships. Everyone among my friends actively cares to some degree about the wellbeing of others. They are willing to reach into their wallets and purses and to volunteer some time and energy for what they believe to be a worthy cause. They do not make a show of their faith, but quietly go about the business of pitching in or reaching out when it seems appropriate. Some do extensive outreach. They ante up to go on mission trips to offer medical or educational help, or to build and repair structures. They never return with a feeling of having been "good." Instead, they tend to return with a feeling of having been privileged to be there.

There is a terrible translation in some of our Bibles that reads, "Be perfect even as your Father in Heaven is perfect." (Matthew 5:48) When the King James Version was translated the term had the proper meaning. I recall a time during an annual conference when a motion was presented and we spent a great deal of time perfecting it. After what seemed an interminable length of time, the bishop inquired, "Do you believe the motion has been perfected?" We agreed. By this the bishop simply meant that everything that was required to act on the motion, if it passed, had been included. The question was called and the motion was overwhelmingly defeated. It was a bad proposal. Still, by Parliamentary rules it was perfect. The times have changed since the days of the King James translation, and our language has changed with the times. That word *perfect* has created much pain and guilt because of the misunderstanding of its meaning. The Greek term, *Teleioi*, which was translated as *perfect*, more accurately means *complete* or *mature* in today's culture. If you read the entire passage and place that phrase in context you clearly see that the call to be complete or mature means in our ability to love as God loves.

I would expand on the understanding of becoming complete to thinking in Jungian terms of *archetypes*. I will make a fuller presentation a bit later. For the moment, let it suffice to say we are a complexity of personalities. We wear some personalities comfortably. Some we try to suppress. Some we never develop properly. Most of us have some inner brokenness that hinders our growth as children of God. Rather than thinking in terms of salvation, I understand our spiritual path as becoming whole, integrating our diverse inner selves into a unified soul.

If this is true, then we must deal with the question of our place and purpose in this amazing, unfathomable universe. We cannot complete the worthy, fully integrated development of every archetypical energy form in our brief lifetime upon this earth. The traditionally offered reward for fulfilling the requirements of the Christian Church is heaven, a place of eternal bliss. I believe this is a gross misunderstanding of God's purpose in creating humanity. It is one that misdirects and retards our development as God's children, made in His image.

Points to Ponder

If the purpose of our faith is not to save us from the judgment of God to deliver us to a place of eternal bliss as opposed to a place of eternal damnation, what purpose does our religious faith serve? Jesus never told his followers to be good. He told them to seek God's Kingdom. He told them to care for others. He told them to trust in God's love and forgiveness. He did not promise them eternal bliss in heaven. He called them to become mature or complete in their ability to give nurturing care to others. Can you find a passage in which he told them they needed to be good?

CHAPTER SEVENTEEN

HEAVEN AND HELL

The basic question any person must answer in order to find any meaning or purpose in life is this: *Was the universe created for a purpose, or did it just randomly occur?*

There is no certain way to prove either possible answer. It is a personal opinion that no one can challenge. It probably is arrived at gradually, based upon life experiences and the influence of people who were significant in one's life. It is useless to attempt to change one's view by logical discourse. Only a change in one's perspective or experience will do this. Frankly, I am weary of quasi intellectuals arguing the case for atheism. The deity they reject is one I rejected long ago. The theology they decry is one I abandoned ages ago. Still, my life experiences convince me that life has a purpose, that this universe is being created in a purposeful manner. It has worked for almost 14 billion years, and continues to expand in a reasonably predictable manner. I feel my own life unfolding, as a seed becomes a plant with buds appearing that eventually will blossom. Whether my choice is true or not I will admit it feels far better than to believe my life is but a random act that ultimately has no meaning. This belief gives roots and direction to my life. It propels me to become more than I am and to create or find some meaning that will survive beyond myself. If our moment in this creation does have purpose, it will not be completed by our spending eternity in heaven or hell. It will be in the fulfillment of the purposes for which we were created. That precludes residing in a place of eternal bliss.

Jesus never talked much about heaven or hell. I assume that this was because he was not much concerned with either. He seemed far more concerned with how we treated one another and what we genuinely felt in our hearts and believed with our minds. Being "saved" did not seem to be an issue of concern for him either.

> *Love the Lord your God with all you heart and all your soul, and all your strength and mind . . . love your neighbor as yourself. For this is the Law and the Prophets.* (Mark 12:30-31)

The Jewish Bible at that time consisted of two sections. The first was the Books of the Law and the second was the writings of the prophets. Effectively Jesus was saying that these two commandments were the summation of all the Scriptures. When you read the sayings of Jesus you will see that his two concerns were that we learn to love God as a caring father rather than to fear him as a wrathful judge, and he wanted us to treat one another with active compassion – regardless of the origin, nationality, status or professed faith of the other person.

However, Jesus did seem to be aware of our levels of moral/ethical development long before modern psychologists began their research. He understood that the lowest form of development is self-centered and operates from a fear of punishment and hope of reward. Frankly I know of only one occasion in which he warns of going to hell. (Matthew 5:22) Jesus speaks often of your Heavenly Father or your Father in heaven. He also speaks of the Kingdom of heaven, but not as a place.[13] The Kingdom of God appears to be more of a state of mind or condition of the soul. [14] The Jewish community had adopted the dualism of Persia and slowly transformed Sheol from a place of eternal sleep into two very diverse final destinations: the place of reward was dubbed *heaven* and the place of punishment was named *hell*. Since heat

---

13 . . . *nor will people say, "Here it is," or "there it is," because the Kingdom of God is within you (or "in your midst.")*. (Luke 17:21)

14 The term "Kingdom of Heaven is only used by Matthew. Mark and Luke use Kingdom of God. It is thought that Matthew, as a godly Jew used Heaven as a pseudonym for God, not wishing to use God's name for fear of using it in vain. This change has caused many to think of *Kingdom of Heaven* as an actual place.

was the enemy of most people in that area, hell was a place of eternal fire and those sent there would burn in hell for eternity. Heaven, by contrast, was a place of beauty and coolness. Scripture gives no clear image of either, but active imaginations of clergy and laity alike have painted many varied pictures of both.

Frankly, when I try to envision a place of eternal peace I have two reactions: The first is, "BORING!" I do not thrive in any environment that has no struggles – no challenges. I become lethargic and listless if there is no stimulus that causes me to think and to act. The conflict of thoughts causes me to explore and understand my own ideas and values. If pushed hard enough I rethink my positions. I learn from the differing views. When I am in a group in which everyone agrees, I learn nothing. I stagnate. There must be some emotional fueling of this process. If the differences do not matter they are of no importance. So in order to have the stimulus to expand my understandings there must be some emotional conflict – and that eliminates eternal peace. I have the distinct belief that most people respond about as I do. Anything resembling eternal peace has a debilitating effect on us. It may sound pleasant when we are caught up in stressful situations. However, most of us recover nicely in a week at the seaside, mountains or cottage. Most of the retirees I know remain active in various ways in order to keep from being bored or having their brains atrophy.

The second reaction is that I am not ready for heaven, nor am I planning on hell. I would mess up heaven for everyone else. In whimsical moments I envision stepping out of the elevator; St. Peter ushers me into a large, glorious room filled with former friends and acquaintances, and introduces me. "Cheatham's here!" someone shouts. "There goes eternal bliss," someone else moans. A few others scurry off to another location. As I said earlier, I do not thrive in an environment that has no struggles. I know I would stir things up just to make myself feel alive (interesting thought) and keep from being bored. My guess is that many of you would have about the same reaction to heaven as a place of eternal bliss.

To think with a bit more depth I do not believe our loving heavenly father spent almost fourteen billion years designing and creating a world in which his children are either eternally rewarded or punished for their behavior during the brief time they spend upon this earth. The idea is even less plausible when you factor in the idea that God gave us free will. If our behavior were that important he would not have done that; God would have prevented any disobedience merely by programing us for obedience.

To me, heaven and hell introduces a terminus in our development as children of God. It is a man-made concept that has no solid biblical foundation. We were created to be God's companions. I do not believe any of us are close to the level of spiritual completeness God intends for us to attain. This misconception of our residing eternally in a place of eternal peace suggests that we humans only have to follow some simple formula in order to gain admission. Once in, always in. I contend that our task in this life is to acquire as complete an understanding of ourselves as possible, in order to become as complete a spiritual being as we can during this journey on earth. This will make our continuing journey easier.

There is one other possibility that I hesitate to suggest. However, it is supported by Scripture and consistent with the events on earth. The principle of "Survival of the Fittest" is well documented by our experiences: the runt of the litter, the frail child, the seedling that did not develop strong roots. As painful as it sometimes is, we know it is a reality of life. Ezekiel 18:4 proclaims: *"The sinful soul shall die."* It may be that those who have badly failed this test of life simply cease to exist. Oblivion: The peace that passes all understanding. Non-existence. Painless . . . but a terrible waste of potential.

Ontological Anxiety and *Ontological Guilt* are deeply embedded forces within us that prod us toward spiritual maturity. On the surface level they cause us to ask such questions as "What should I be doing with my life?" They cause us to feel uneasy, even with attained success, and to reach for more. When misguided by society's mores and values they lead us astray. We may climb more ladders and attain more symbols of success, but remain dissatisfied with where we are in our life's journey.

It has been said that outer space is our greatest and last frontier. I suggest that *inner* space is that frontier. The end of the nineteenth century ushered in the beginning of this exploration with the introduction of the fledgling science of psychology. This was about the same time when an active interest in aeronautics also began. One led us toward the outer universe. The other led us toward the inner mystery of the self.[15]

When we stop blaming Satan or finding scapegoats to explain and blame for our problems, and then begin to address them honestly, we open the door to resolving them. As long as we blame others we place ourselves in the role of *victims*. Victims have no control over their lives. They have lost the power to determine who they are, what they do, and what they will become. Those who live in this mode require a savior. They are dependent on others or another to give their lives meaning and direction. I do not choose to live my life as a victim. Jesus of Nazareth never suggested that we should. "You are the light of the world. Let your light shine." (Matthew 5: 16) does not sound like a command to be dependent. The entire list of Beatitudes (Matthew 5:1 -12) suggests action on our part.

Even as we begin this process of becoming more like the Man of Galilee we desire to know and to follow, we would do well to answer this question: Why do we wish to become like Jesus or to follow him? What is to be gained by being a Christian? For most people who call themselves "Christians," their faith really has not caused them to be distinguished from their non-Christian neighbors. They appear to be decent, hard working people living happy, productive lives, but they are not necessarily more generous of spirit, more accepting of differences, more forgiving of others, and more concerned for the poor and the outcasts of society. In short, their resemblance to the person they call the Lord of their lives is no greater than their neighbor who never attended a Christian worship service . . . or the neighbor who follows a non-Christian faith.

I have two primary reasons for my decision: The first is selfish. I once read a statement by journalist Sydney J. Harris in which he spoke about how people would respond if they really knew what was good for them. He took the long view in explaining what he meant. I have no recollection of where this was printed, but it does remain indelibly embossed in my mind. Since I believe in a deity who has an eternal plan for us as companions, and I know I am nowhere near being prepared for this role, I realize I had best work

15 This is a term Carl Jung used to define the hidden inner dimension of ourselves we might call our soul.

toward that end, and Jesus is my best model. With the passing of the years I have come to realize that many of those things I pursued in younger days were of far lesser value than what I ignored. As I reflect over the years lived I am aware that I found (and still find) far greater joy and satisfaction over the gifts I have given (in all their various forms) than in those I have received. It is as though God has implanted some quality within us that responds more positively to the closed hand that opens to give, than the open hand that closes to grasp.

There is another dimension to that which factors into my thinking. Einstein's Theory of relativity has been demonstrated to be accurate. It no longer is a theory, but an accepted principle of physics that neither time nor space has an absolute value. They exist in order for matter to exist. I believe that when the soul departs this physical world it departs the realm of time and space and exists in a dimension such as our Creator resided prior to what scientists call "The Big Bang" and the Book of Genesis says, "In the beginning." In such a dimension neither time nor space exists, and all relationships will be spiritual relationships. We will be more closely related to those who are spiritual like ourselves. I recall the Great Judgment in Matthew 25: 31-46, when those who demonstrated active nurturing care for the needy were called to be with God, and those who ignored the cries of the needy were banished into the darkness. The thought of being eternally separated from my loving Father throughout eternity, quite frankly, is another one of those "self-interest" factors.

To do that which I believe is best for me has transformed my priorities and urges me on to become one who follows Jesus more closely.

The other reason is a simple one of loving response. Whenever I reflect upon the wonder of this gift of life – the rich experiences: love, friendship, successes, moments of intimacy of body and mind, the beauties of sound, sight, and smell, the tenderness and thrill of touch, the delights of taste . . . and countless more - I am overwhelmed with gratitude and love for the One who made all this possible. So if this One we call Father wants me to become far more than I now am, that is reason enough for me.

Like most who wish to be Christians in fact as well as in name, I had no intention of being radical about it. More caring, more generous of spirit (but don't overdo it), more forgiving and more involved with the poor and the outcast (but, again, don't overdo it). That seemed to be just the right balance for me. The catch was that once any of us decides to take up that cross and start following the Man of Galilee, we have no idea where that road will lead us. I suppose a bit of that depends upon how serious we actually are about being a loyal follower. That, in turns, depends upon how deep our belief (call it faith, if you will) that this Jesus is the real thing – the one anointed by God to show us the clear path to a lasting relationship with God himself. If that really is what we believe, then anything less than a total commitment is foolish and shortsighted.

Points to Ponder

I will leave it to you to determine your present level of commitment and the degree to which you will dedicate some time and energy to your quest. What I will share with you offers many different levels of response. You may use some of the tools and suggestions to sharpen your life, make it work easier and better. This follows what I believe was the typical response of those who sat on the hillsides and actually heard Jesus teach. You can use the material as a gateway to greater involvement, finding yourself more deeply invested in your community and even beyond. I believe this represents the level of many who followed him as disciples, but were not a part of The Twelve, the inner group who knew him intimately. Those whose present commitment equals that of The Twelve have already traveled beyond the scope of this book. If you read the Scriptures carefully and thoughtfully you know that those Twelve did not begin with the commitment they displayed after the resurrection, so take heart. I believe those Twelve were at a time in their lives when Jesus could easily detect the hunger in their eyes. His call to abandon their work and follow him was heard through eager ears. Wherever you are on your journey, this next section will be of value.

SECTION THREE

REPENTANCE

Do not be conformed to this world, but be transformed by the renewal of your mind, that by testing you may discern what is the will of God, what is good and acceptable and perfect. (Romans 12:2)

What does the term Repent mean to you? My guess is that your understanding of the word is quite different from the way in which Jesus and his early followers used it.

The original meaning of this biblical term, *Repent!* has been lost – or at least badly distorted. Under the negative influence of the medieval Church and later Calvinism, it now carries the terrible connotation of negative judgment. Many years ago, I was engaged in a three way theological conversation with two bright, young clergy. Dick was Episcopalian and Bob was Presbyterian. At a certain point I felt myself at odds with Bob, which was strange because we seemed to be in accord on almost every theological, social and political issue. It was Dick who first spoke up and inquired as to what was happening. Bob said he could not use the term *Repent* easily because it carried a sense of the individual already having been condemned. I was using it as a hopeful invitation. As we pursued our different interpretations I realized that Bob was drawing from his Calvinist roots and I was drawing from Jesus. "Jesus never would have called us to repent if it was not possible for us to do so," I explained. Then we went back to the root meaning of the term.

Typically we hear that *repent* means to turn around. This may occur as a result of genuine repentance, but it is not the meaning of the term. Those who pretend to understand Greek may say it means to change your mind. This falls far short of the meaning. The Greek word we translate as repent is *metanoia*. It is composed of two more-basic terms: *meta* and *noia* (or *nous*). Meta denotes transformation as in metamorphous. Nous denotes the function of the mind. It incorporates the idea of perspective as well as thought. To more completely define the term requires a sentence: "After thoughtful consideration, radically transform the manner in which you perceive, understand and think about everything." Matthew sets the tone for this necessary radical transformation by putting the condensed bulk of Jesus' sayings at the beginning of his Gospel account, "The Sermon on the Mount."

The Beatitudes fly in the face of society's values: Blessed (fortunate) are the poor in spirit, who mourn, who are gentle, who hunger and thirst for righteousness, who are merciful, pure in heart, peacemakers, and have been persecuted and slandered. Can you imagine the stunned response of those who first heard these words? They ran contrary to the values of their society. Yet, they must have had a subterranean ring of truth somewhere inside of them, or the crowds would not have remained, nor followed him, not called him rabbi (teacher).

Jesus proclaimed that we should love our enemy, turn the other cheek when hit, go an extra distance for the Roman soldier who forces people to carry his burden, pray for the people who would abuse us. Then Jesus goes further by claiming that our righteousness must exceed that of the Pharisees' actions, and even then our actions mean nothing unless they are genuinely from our hearts.

Had I been there, listening to him, I would have been overwhelmed by the audacity and extravagance of his message. To even begin to live in accordance with those demands would require a complete makeover of my mind . . . and soul. If I were to take him seriously I would quickly realize it was an all or nothing deal he offered. For some people, this transformation is a gradual process. There was no moment when they would say, "Ah ha, I understand it!" Or to use a traditional phrase, "This was the moment when I was saved." Their temperament, environment and experience cooperated to create a lifestyle of steady progress along their spiritual journey. For others, like Paul, there may have been a flash of overwhelming insight that jumpstarted a rapid movement along their newly-found path.

Mark begins his gospel with Jesus proclaiming: "The time is fulfilled, and the Kingdom of God is at hand: repent and believe the gospel." (Mark 1:15). Essentially Mark claims Jesus said, "Everything is ready and God's Kingdom is here for you. All you have to do is believe that, then transform the whole way you have looked at life, and you will become God's people – not Herod's or Caesar's."

I believe Jesus' call has the same sense of immediacy today as when he first uttered it. God's Kingdom is not a future hope that will wondrously appear as a magical Disneyland. It is a present reality and a present possibility for every living soul. We have just to want it enough to make its attainment our major priority. This does not mean one must abandon all other activities or make major sacrifices of time. It simply means you must be willing to rearrange the priorities of your life to conform to the demands of God. You must be willing to do the work necessary to effect a metamorphous of the mind. As the change occurs your priorities of time and energy will change as a matter of course. There is no thirty or ninety day fix. Repentance, in its original and finest sense, requires a lifetime and beyond. It is a spiritual journey that is comparable to the great physical journeys made by those who traveled the ocean to come to America. Many had to learn a new language. All had to let go of their past in order to build a worthy future. Essentially each new pilgrim had to learn a new style of living. Some made the transition easily. Some struggled for years. Some, as a matter of reality, never truly made the adjustment and lived as exiles, mouthing words they never believed or actualized in their lives. However, every major step forward in this spiritual pilgrimage will result in a greater sense of wholeness, connectedness and worthy purposefulness in your life. It will be worth every moment you devote to it.

Remember throughout this section that my basic premise is that God's purpose for creating you and me – and all of humanity – is that we are to be God's companions. God, the supreme Lover, has created us to love and be loved. As an essential part of being "lovers of God," we will naturally share this love with all of God's children. It will not be a matter of should or ought. By the very nature of who we become through the metamorphosis of our soul, it will be the expected fruit of our lives. As there is no quick fix, there also is no simple formula. Paul said it well: ". . . you must work out your own salvation in fear and trembling." (Philippians 2:12)

From my entry into the ordained ministry in the early 60's, I have done my best to dig beneath the surface of our theology to understand the dynamics of what it means to be human. Outward forms and expressions change over time, but the essential qualities of being human remain constant. Terms like repentance, conversion, salvation and even Christian love have no meaning unless I understand how those terms translate themselves into attitudes and actions I can perform. I also have reached into the various disciplines of science to understand this creation more fully. I believe the more we know about our world, the clearer our understanding of God and God's nature and purpose will be. Consequently, I have studied and blended the disciplines of psychology, sociology, history, quantum physics, astronomy and a smattering of a few others to form my framework for doing theology. There are a variety of systems for understanding and altering our inner nature. Every system falls short simply because we humans are very complex creatures. We still are in the early stages of understanding the human psyche. A question I continue to wrestle with is the source of thought. A computer is capable of manipulating symbols with far more accuracy, complexity and speed than I, but it has no ability to generate thought – to have an idea emerge into a realm where it could deal with it by itself. Yet we humans are constantly bombarded with thoughts we never consciously attempt to create or review. Our minds operate like primitive computers in regards to their ability to deal with whatever thoughts we have. Yet these sluggish computers we call our minds can do what even the most sophisticated computers cannot accomplish: they generate ideas, create and synthesize relevant thoughts. When our nation set a goal of landing a man on the moon we thought of space as our last great frontier. However, I suggest that inner space – the human psyche – is that last, greatest frontier. Until we learn how to understand and control that area none of our efforts at progress will bear its potential of worthy fruit.

There are many brilliant people pursuing this understanding. I do not pretend to be among them. I am but a simple theologian who uses their tools to help me in my quest for God. I have found that a mixture of the psychological schools I will present work fairly well for my journey to wholeness. Bear in mind throughout this presentation that terms like *ego, id* and *archetype* do not represent an actual reality that could be located within a person. Rather, they are terms that serve to define certain common characteristics of human behavior and inner dynamics. Different psychological schools use different terms because they have constructed different models for analyzing human behavior. Freud, for example, would use the term *libido*, where Berne might speak of the *natural child*.

A final reminder before we explore some of these psychological schools: I present them as models that are useful in understanding the inner workings of our minds. *The ultimate purpose of this section is to assist you, the reader, in developing an understanding and method for actually working out your own salvation.* Repentance, the transformation of your mental process is neither an easy nor short-term task.

Chapter Eighteen

The Elephant and the Rider

In my eclectic reading, I once encountered a book I wished had been required reading at my seminary. It had not been written at that time, however. Its title is *The Happiness Hypothesis.* The author, Jonathan Haidt, uses a simple model to explain Paul's dilemma: "For I do not do the good I want to do; no, the evil I do not want to do – I keep on doing." (Romans 7:15)

Dr. Haidt proposes that we think of the more primitive portion of the brain, the amygdala, as *the elephant,* and we consider the rational part, the cerebral cortex lobes, as *the rider.* The rider can cause the elephant to take him wherever he wishes to go . . . *as long as the elephant also is willing to go to that same place.* If the elephant refuses or resists, then the rider must force the elephant by any means he can muster. For all practical purposes, the most common means is what we call *will power.* The rider must impose his will upon his more basic instincts in order to achieve his goal. The amygdala controls our most primitive instincts for our survival as individuals and as a species. It has the power to override whatever the rational portion considers to be the proper course of action. Whenever a situation arises that calls for immediate reaction, the stimulus bypasses the normal route of passage through the brain and takes a shortcut directly to the amygdala. This is the reason many of us suffer what I call "The Vesuvian Complex." We erupt immediately and then quiet down when the stimulus reaches our more thoughtful areas of the brain. These survival instincts not only include fear and anger (flight or fight) but such drives as sexual reproduction.

This is the primary reason Paul – and the rest of us – have problems trying to follow our *"shoulds"* and *"oughts."* It is the reason our New Year's resolutions are discarded by February. The rider simply wears out from trying to control the elephant. I do not recall a statement in Scripture that tells of Jesus directly ordering his followers to do good things or to avoid doing bad things. He called them to become whole or worthy as persons, knowing the good would flow naturally from who they were at their core.

When my daughters were in their late teens they once shared their belief that I had given them some hang ups along the way. I recall acknowledging that this probably was true. Then I added, "I could only do who I was at that time." It was not "I did the best I could." For me it was more basic. *I did who I was.* In the long run we can never do more. Our task in life then is to grow into the fullness of the image of God in order to produce better fruit. There are exceptions, of course, but a good rule of thumb is this: if you want happier, more productive children, then you should become a happier, more productive parent. To this end I have learned to focus more on the elephant than the rider. I also have learned that the carrot (reward) is more effective than the stick (punishment) in effecting significant and lasting change. Good trainers understand and love their animals. Effective spiritual pilgrims learn to understand and love their inner elephants. Dispense with the notion that Satan is whispering in your ear and enticing you to sin. I believe Paul would have been more successful with his inward struggles if he had ceased attempting to suppress his urges and learned to recognize and own them, and therefore had been able to exercise some control over them. Of course, Paul did not have the advantage of the psychological insights available to us today.

Some while back I realized that people do not become what they are told to become. They tend to become what they are told they *are.* A good teacher never tells students they are bad, slow, sloppy, poor – or any other negative label. A good teacher identifies students' strengths and begins drawing and developing those qualities – praising as the students progress. By the same token I believe any preacher worthy of the title never – NEVER – tells his people they are sinners. Sinning (falling short of the moral/ethical standard) is something most of us *do* from time to time. That, however, is not who we *are.* Jesus constantly spoke of God as "Your heavenly father." If God is, in fact, our father, then we – all of us – must be God's children, created in His image. *That* is our nature. Every part of you – those parts you try to hide – of which you are ashamed – are portions of the divine image that have been broken and fragmented – misdirected – and displaced. They are not to be locked up and hidden. They are to be called out into the light to be acknowledged, loved, healed, affirmed and integrated into the whole of you. Every inner, focused-energy that resides within you has been given by God and serves a useful purpose if placed in the light and guided by love.

This elephant roaming inside of you can become a great force for good, if loved and properly trained. But it will take work – work, patience and skill. Elephant riders are trained. Some have more talent but none become qualified riders without acquiring the necessary skills. I have learned that a workable way of changing the elephant's priorities is through practical experience. We may spend innumerable hours discussing ethics and moral values in a classroom without it affecting our actions. In fact, I have observed that voicing the proper thoughts too often serves as a substitute for acting on them. I agree with James on the issue of faith and action:

What good is it, my brothers, if a person claims to have faith but has no deeds? Can such faith save him? Suppose a brother or sister is without clothes or daily food. If one of you says to him, "Go, I wish you well. Keep warm and fed," but does nothing about his physical needs, what good is that? In the same way, faith by itself, unaccompanied by action, is dead. But someone will say, "You have faith; I have deeds." Show me your faith without deeds, and I will show you my faith by my deeds. You believe there is one God. Good! Even the demons believe that and shudder. You foolish person, do you want evidence that faith without deeds is useless?" (James 2:14-20)

In our better moments we have the opportunity to devise practices and systems for protecting ourselves from our worse moments and for becoming more than we presently are. It is in living our higher ideals that we change; therefore it follows that would-be followers of Jesus should find ways of doing so. As I review my personal journey I realize that many growth experiences were planned, but many were serendipitous. I either inserted myself or found myself in a situation that demanded I grow, or by its nature generated the change.

The most powerful experience I had during my seminary years was a three-month stint as a student chaplain intern at the University of Michigan Hospital in Ann Arbor. We spent the first two weeks as orderlies in the wards. The reason was two-fold: this gave us the opportunity to learn how the hospital worked. It also gave us the opportunity to observe how wards functioned while virtually unseen (no one notices orderlies). We quickly realized that the dynamics of a ward changed when someone wearing a short, white jacket with a cross on it appeared. At first I felt discounted, downgraded. "Here I am – a college graduate doing menial labor. This is not what I signed up for," I mumbled to myself. Then I was given the assignment of changing a bed – with a patient still in it. Whatever plan I had in my head fell miserably short when I actually tried to implement it. The patient, a thin, older man, lay patiently while I made a few failed attempts. Finally he held up his hand to stop me, climbed out of the bed, and sat himself on a nearby chair to be out of harm's way. As I continued to struggle with the now-empty bed, he said gently, "Don't worry, young man, you'll get the hang of it." Then he went on to explain that he had been an employee of the hospital for decades. I felt like a fool – worse than a fool! I was a snob and a fool! I who thought I was above menial labor because I had spent four years in a college, could not even perform the most fundamental task of a hospital orderly. This kindly gentleman did not criticize me. He offered encouragement. He understood how difficult it is to learn all the requirements of any job. In many ways I learned more that was useful from this older gentleman in that brief moment than I had been taught by some PhDs in an entire semester. As an unseen orderly I observed the wards operating as caring communities. Some got out of their beds and dragged their medical paraphernalia across the room to comfort or pour water for someone they had never met. Some struggled over to an adjacent bed to speak a word of comfort or to hold hands and pray. When I put on my short, white jacket and ministered to some in the expensive, private rooms I usually found the patient, alone and bored. I had to wonder why they chose to be alone. We are more human – more fully alive - when we are in community.

Under the pressure of the supervisors' counseling I became aware of the many ways we have of avoiding genuine intimacy with one another. We avoid issues we believe to be too personal. We switch subjects when any issue feels uncomfortable. The tone of our voice signals when we prefer to stay on the surface and merely chitchat, rather than to speak of the important issues that burn inside of us. One by one, my "sadistic" supervisors stripped away my long-established defenses and made me vulnerable enough to be of some value to those I wished to serve. Some defenses have restored themselves, of course, but I now know how to remove them when the situation calls for depth and honesty.

The Steven Ministry program offers a wonderful opportunity to thrust yourself into situations that require and cause you to grow spiritually. Steven Ministers are laypersons who have taken specialized training to help people who are in a difficult time in their lives. I could give a plethora of examples where volunteers with only a desire to help others found themselves enriched beyond their wildest expectations as they shared themselves with someone caught in a time of crisis. Their tasks were simply to be the supportive, caring confidants of some person or some family that was going through difficult times. There were sicknesses, divorces, suicides, deaths, abandonment, abuse, empty-nests – you name it; these Steven ministers experienced it. Their compassion overrode their fears and feelings of inadequacy. They not only helped others, but helped themselves along their spiritual journey in the process.

Some people who volunteered to work at soup kitchens discovered inner dimensions they never suspected existed. Others made similar discoveries as volunteer tutors, drivers, camp counselors, church schoolteachers, or any number of other tasks that help fill in the holes of society to make it work. Any task that puts you in a servant role, tending to the needs of others, sets you walking in the path of those fishermen who walked with Jesus. There should not be any sense of having done something special. Rather, there is a simple sense of quiet joy – or contentment – that pleases the elephant as greatly as it does the rider. Once that occurs the journey becomes easier.

Shoulds and oughts do not beget lasting transformations of the soul. The actual experience of "blessed are the humble, the poor in spirit, the peacemakers, the ones willing to mourn" is what generates the repentance to which Jesus gave the invitation.

Chapter Nineteen

Who's in Charge?

I am fascinated by the stories of multiple personalities. I devoured *The Three Faces of Eve,*[1] Then *Sybil*[2] was published, and I could barely put it down. I have always resonated to the words of the Gerasene demoniac in Mark 5:9 who, when asked his name, replied, "They call me Legion, for I am many." I am aware of the different varieties of "me" that reside in myself: the jock, the student, the musician, the Boy Scout, the comedian, the prankster, the teacher, the lover – and many, many others whose ego allows them to blend in and out seamlessly. Reading about Eve and Sybil helped me understand that only a strong ego holds them together. By the time I had encountered *The Many Minds of Billy Milligan*[3] I had done some reading on Jungian archetypes and began to grasp the depth and extent of the human personality. The personalities within Billy were similar to the archetypes.

Assembled within each of us is a multitude of personalities, or focused energy sources, held together by a sense of self we call "The Ego." Carl Jung, the noted Swiss psychiatrist, called those personalities Archetypes. In the course of a typical day many of these archetypes appear and disappear as called for by the central archetype we call th*e Ruler.* From time to time the Jester may appear to ease a situation with humor. If there is a challenge it may elicit the

1 Thispen, Corbett, *The Three Faces of Eve*, London: Seeker & Warburg, 1957

2 Schreiber, Flora, *Sybil,* New York: Warner Book, Inc., 1974

3 Keys, Daniel, *The Many Minds of Billy Milligan,* New York: Bantam Books, *1982* .

Warrior, or – better yet – the Magician. The Warrior confronts and is ready for a fight. The Magician has a way of transforming the situation and easing the tension without either backing down or generating anger. Carol Pearson has done some excellent work in defining some primary archetypes. I recommend her book, *Awakening the Heroes Within*,[4] as an excellent introductory work. It is the clearest exposition of archetypes I have encountered. Years ago I was fortunate enough to stumble into one of her classes during a national meeting of the Association of Psychological Types (APT). I immediately recognized that her approach offered an excellent guide to spiritual growth.

Those of you who are unfamiliar with the idea of archetypes might find it easier to think of them as aspects of our personality. There is a part of you that is serious and another aspect that is playful. There is a part of you that is creative. There is an aspect of you that is cautious and another that may be curious and venturesome. There is a dimension of you that is caring and another that is more preoccupied with your own needs and concerns. We are a multiplicity of different dimensions of what it means to be human. Emotionally healthy and stable people move unconsciously and effortlessly through these various aspects as a matter of course. For those wishing to make major changes in the way they perceive life, it is helpful to be aware of these aspects or archetypes. Therefore, I give you this brief introduction to this awareness in order to provide you with another tool for repenting in the manner Jesus offered us. By repenting, I mean redirecting your current life path, and walking, talking and acting as a true follower of Jesus.

The point I make here is that every dimension of our being is God-given. We are made in God's image and each part of us is potentially godly. Society tends to distort some of these aspects and we try to dismiss them. In doing so, we push them over to the dark side, hiding them, in as much as possible, from our own self. Check yourself on these points: those who are parents become most upset with our children when we see the traits in them we dislike and try to deny within ourselves. All of us tend to dislike those same traits in others we know. Jesus said something about "Judge not that you might not be judged, for with the judgment you make you, yourself, will be judged." (Matthew 7:1) I understand this to mean that when you negatively

4 Pearson, Carol, *Awakening The Hero Within, San Francisco, 1991*

judge another person you often are saying more about yourself than about the person you demean.

I have been in groups where some newcomers have personality traits that are annoying to others. In the better groups those persons are welcomed, treated well, and eventually loved. In the course of this process they are changed. They become more pleasant, more cooperative . . . more caring for the members of the group. Essentially they are transformed by love. I wanted my children to be all the good things they had the qualities to become, not because they feared me or wanted a reward, but simply because they loved me and wanted to express that love in a manner that pleased me. That is the worthy and lasting reason I wished to offer them. They responded far better than I deserved. This inner family of ours reacts best when treated the same way. In 1976, I saw a movie entitled Sybil. It was a docudrama based upon the book about a young lady with a multiple personality disorder. The ending scene was one that could not have been written into the book. It showed Sybil, now with a healed ego strong enough to integrate her many personalities, sitting on a lush, grassy lawn. As each of her broken parts approached her, Sybil extended her arms to accept them and hug them lovingly back into her now almost complete self. The last, a young girl named Peggy, hid fearfully behind a tree. Peggy was the one who had suffered most from her mother's abuse. She carried anger and was a bit of a rebel. When Peggy peeked out from behind a tree, Sybil smiled and beckoned her to come. Shyly, fearfully, Peggy slowly approached, not certain she would be accepted. Finally when she was near enough, Sybil reached out to embrace her, much as the Prodigal's father reached out to embrace his lost son. The audience watched Peggy slowly, lovingly disappear into her place with Sybil who now was complete – whole. The scene was a metaphor, of course. The actual process had required months of hard work. Still, that is much the process each of us needs to follow if we, too, are to become complete – or *perfect* – to use the outdated term found in older translations of Scripture.

I will offer a few examples of archetypes interacting within the individual. It will sound strange, but bear with me please. First, I will give some snapshot summaries of different personalities within Billy Milligan, as they conveyed their experiences to the author of the book.

When asked to describe what his experience within Billy was, one of the personalities compared it with lying on a large, darkened stage, vaguely aware of what was occurring "above." Suddenly the spotlight was on him and he knew he had to perform. He improvised his time in the limelight and then found himself lying on the darkened stage again. Some personalities spoke of "losing time." They were unaware of the others, but found themselves leaving for work on a Tuesday and suddenly being aware that it was Thursday and they were returning home. A few believed they had roommates, but never actually saw them. It seemed that each worked out for himself or herself (Billy had a few feminine personalities) their understanding of their disconnected lives.

With that in mind, let's see how a healthy, connected family of archetypes functions during a normal day.

Melinda's Jock is an early riser who hops out of bed and immediately begins to bustle about, preparing for the day. Her Ruler has learned to focus and organize the day, so she has allowed herself the extra time to do so. Before beginning the process of washing and dressing, while still in the jock mode, she does some basic stretching and light exercise. As she showers, her Ruler begins to outline the activities of the day while the Caregiver handles the showering and dressing and insures that she is thoroughly clean, and pampers her a bit as she places every hair properly before spraying and adding her make up. At breakfast her Jester decides to sprinkle some coconut flakes on the cereal to give it a bit of extra zest. Then her Magician leads her to "The Chair" where she spends five minutes in quiet meditation, centering herself on the simple mantra she found in Philippians 4:13: *"I can do all things through the one who empowers me."*[5] Her Warrior lifts the cell phone from its charger, places it in her purse and heads for her car. As she backs from the garage, her Sage reminds her that she has plenty of time to arrive at work successfully. Her Warrior has heard this many times and is a bit disgusted, but heeds the advice and drives, aggressively, but with care.

5 This is the literal translation of the Greek that has no mention of Christos in it. Also, the Greek *dynamos,* in this instance, best translates as *empowers.*

While driving, her Lover (who is a romantic) reflects upon Greg, whom she has been dating now for six months. She recalls one special evening and momentarily allows herself to relive the emotions. Even though her conscious mind dwells on this, her Warrior continues to maneuver the car safely along the streets. Her Ruler is aware, however, that unless she consciously focuses on her driving she will go past her exit, so the Ruler interrupts Melinda's reverie to let her focus on the driving.

At work, her Caregiver emerges to greet the employees in her department. She inquires how each is feeling and how their families are doing. There is nothing artificial in this. Melinda's Caregiver is thoroughly integrated into her personality, and she is a caring person. Melinda is the department head and remembers how her predecessor greeted everyone and emotionally drew them together each morning. When she had been promoted she initially began copying her predecessor's practice, but it soon became quite natural. There were times when Melinda quietly gave thanks for the excellent athletic program she had in high school. Without realizing it she had learned how to develop her Warrior properly, playing by the rules and leaving the Warrior on the playing field. Because of that experience she is comfortable with her role as a department head. She had seen so many girls who had not participated in athletics or taken advantage of other "warrior-growth" opportunities. Their undeveloped warrior archetypes became shadow warriors who took out their aggressiveness with spiteful words. Even in high school she had learned to avoid them because of the hurtful gossip.

During the day Melinda seamlessly switched aspects (or archetypes) of her personality. When a customer shared a family loss, both her Orphan and Caregiver appeared: one to mourn with her, and the other to offer comfort. There was nothing phony about either because Melinda had experienced loss and understood the pain. Sometimes her Magician stepped forward when an irate customer confronted one of her salespersons. She had long-ago learned that her Warrior needed to stay on the bench and let The Magician transform the situation and resolve the issue peacefully. There were moments when her Jester appeared to laugh and be playful. At times, her Innocent looked about and realized how very fortunate she was to be where she was at this point in her life. "Life, indeed, is good," she would tell herself. Her Creator would come up with an idea for how to display a new product, and her Destroyer would find a way to stop displaying a poorly selling product to make space for it. Sometimes at home, these two archetypes worked together to rework her schedule or make room for a new piece of furniture. Melinda had learned to use these two as a team. If she wanted to add something to her life or her home she also needed to remove something. Otherwise her life or home would become cluttered.

At lunchtime, Melinda always found a few quiet moments for meditation, once again repeating a mantra. Sometimes it was a simple, "I thank you, Lord, for your presence in my life." Some days, when the morning was hectic she used her coffee break for meditating. "Much more refreshing," she told herself. On the way home, her Lover often emerged once the car was safely in traffic. At times her Lover planned with her Creator for her Friday evening candlelight dinner with Greg. Once home, depending on the day, her Orphan might have heaved a sigh of relief, her Jester may have turned on some music and danced, or her Sage may have reached for a book, a cool drink and settled into a chair.

All of the day's events flowed together within one personality having absolutely no sense of different aspects entering and exiting because the strong ego held them together. However, if the Ruler had not been strong, the Warrior may have missed the exit or tried to intervene when she should have remained on the bench. It takes a strong, mature team to bring off a worthy life. When one of the important actors is missing or inept, or if the Ruler is not in charge, life does not work well and the individual has no clue as to why it does not. In the case of Billy Milligan it was called "Mix-up time." No one was in charge, and whoever appeared – appeared. The shadow personalities erupted and misbehaved, which is why Billy ended up in the penitentiary. Incidentally, I have seen "normal" people who had no one – or wrong one – in charge of their lives and they strike me as the ones the philosopher Soren Kierkegaard was referring to when he spoke of those living their lives in quiet desperation. When Warriors are in charge, and too often they are, they tend to create win/lose situations. They are overly competitive and know little of diplomacy. If there is no mature Caregiver children are ignored, even abused and neglected . . . including one's own Inner Child. We have all seen those stern characters who have no Jester. Life is humorless for them. Mood changing drugs, from alcohol to harder types, have a way of displacing the Ruler and giving free rein to shadow types.

There are two ways of understanding our shadow: one is the shadow archetypes and the other draws from the school of typology that covers a broader, less defined quality. Perhaps it is time for me to confess an embarrassing discovery. I am what is termed an Intuitor. I draw from my intuition more than from direct sensory experience. Intuitors tend to be creative by nature. When I found my creativity drying up I often became interested (almost to the point of obsession) in some item that previously held little interest for me. I would begin reading what I could on the subject. I even spent time in malls or showrooms searching for information of styles, and I am one who does not like to shop. Often I ended up purchasing the item for which I had little or no useful purpose. Eventually I began to recognize the pattern: I had fallen into my Sensing shadow. I knew it was a shadow because what I was doing was either non-productive or counter-productive. *That* always is a sure sign that your shadow is in charge. I decided to handle that issue in what for me was the simplest and most effective manner. Whenever I realized my Sensing shadow was operating I put on my running suit, donned my running shoes and spent the time I otherwise would have wasted running in the park. Two things, both positive, resulted: I got in better physical condition, and the shadow more quickly gave way to a return of the positive dimension of my Intuition. You might check yourself to see the pattern you take when your shadow springs forth. Remember, the results always are useless at best.

Another dimension of shadow is when any of our archetypes has ceased acting in a positive manner and has taken on the negative qualities of that archetype. This often takes the form of addictive non-productive behavior. Drugs, alcohol, pornography are the most publicized addictions, but there are many more, and some are as destructive as those three. Busyness addiction is the most prevalent in the United States. It takes many forms in us. When it was first recognized, people called it workaholism. With time it was recognized to run far beyond that. The end purpose of any addiction is to avoid intimacy - with oneself as well as with others. When we are immersed in an activity we do not have time to think of ourselves or to spend time with others. Reading, television, games, hobbies – practically any activity - can become addictive. That behavior can be just your shadows trying to hide from themselves and from others.

The other form of shadow can be that aspect of yourself that has crossed over to the dark side. Your Warrior may be acting as a terrorist, needlessly attacking others in order to feel in charge or to act out some anger that festers deep within yourself. Your Caregiver may have become an enabler to feel indispensible, loved or in charge. Your Orphan – rather than learning to become interdependent and sympathetic - may have become a "Help Me" case. Your Jester may have become a frivolous fool, incapable of being serious or useful. We all have some aspect of a shadow personality operating within us. We may be able to keep it under control so long as we are under control. Alcohol or stress may cause us to lose control, however. We have heard many a person lament, "I just wasn't myself," after sobering up or removing the stress. This shadow may have been in charge for hours, weeks, months or in some cases – years.

We do not control our shadows by trying to keep them exiled. As mentioned earlier, we must learn to love them and transform them. I have learned that light and love can do this if there is genuine desire to do so. Name them and draw them into the light. Then loving support can do wonders in rehabilitating these lost, broken parts of you. "Be ye perfect (complete – whole)" is an invitation given by Jesus. (Matthew 5:48)

I believe Jesus was a perfect model for how our archetypes should operate: His Ruler was (almost) always in control. The only time I recall a loss of control was when he was unexpectedly confronted by the Syro-Phoenician woman reported in Mark 7:24-30. His deeply embedded racial prejudice jumped up and he insulted her. Immediately, however, he regained control and acted in his normal, caring manner. He rarely displayed the aggressive part of his Warrior. Still, it was his Warrior courage that carried him throughout his ministry. He never was afraid of confrontation or of speaking the truth. Caregiver, Sage and Magician were obviously balanced and mature. It was his Jester or Fool who enjoyed banquets and had the sense of humor. The balance between his Innocent and his Orphan also was obvious. The person who told us to trust in God to provide for our needs was the same person who said, "The Son of Man has no place to lay his head." (Luke 9:58)

A story I heard somewhere in my studies was about a small village which was being terrorized by a dragon. On occasion, the dragon would roam into the village breathing fire, burning buildings and frightening the people. Immediately the village Warrior leaped into action and engaged the dragon, only to be badly burned and retire in defeat. Other members of the village made attempts to subdue the dragon, but they failed as well. Finally the Ruler of the village decided to engage the dragon in conversation rather than with weapons. "Why are you burning the village?" he inquired. "It's my nature to breathe fire," the dragon responded. The Ruler thought for a moment. Then he smiled and gestured to the dragon: "Follow me," he said. "I believe I have just the job for you." He led the dragon to the edge of town where there was a huge trash pile. It was the village dumping ground. "The trash has been piling up and the stench is terrible," he said. "Would you care to help us?" he asked. The dragon nodded his assent, so the Ruler led the dragon to the far edge. "You can be our chief incinerator," he proclaimed. And as the story went: "They all lived happily ever after." We all have some inner dragon or dragons roaming around within us. Your inner dragons are a part of you. Rather than blaming them or fighting them, learn how to put them to use.

Again, I recommend Carol Pearson's book, *Awakening the Heroes Within,* for those who wish to learn more of this dynamic we call *archetypes.* In any event, I suggest you take an honest look and ask yourself who is in charge of your inner family. A wise Ruler who resembles the person of Jesus is the one to make your life work as a child of God. Intentionally affirm your Ruler in the morning to start your day. There are too many dysfunctional internal families operating in our society, where the Warrior, Trickster, Orphan, Destroyer, Lover-turned-Predator – or no one in particular runs the show. The decisions are faulty, but the person never realizes it and wonders why life does not work well. He may spend much time in fantasy, or non-productive activity, buying lottery tickets in hopes of becoming successful. If any of these scenarios sound like you I recommend you find a competent Jungian psychologist to help get you on track. Jesus is our model, but ultimately each of us is responsible for our own lives. We are the only ones who can live it. We are the ones who must bear the consequences of our decisions.

Eric Berne created a different model for understanding our inner being. He developed the school we call Transactional Analysis. Its purpose was to help us understand the dynamics of the transactions we have *between* ourselves and *within* ourselves. He employed a simple model of Parent, Adult and Child. The Parent he divides into Nurturing Parent and Critical Parent and the child is divided into Adapted Child and Natural Child. Those familiar with archetypes may read nuances into this model, but it works quite well for its purpose. The ground rules are these:

A Critical Parent can only interact with another Critical Parent or an Adapted Child.

A Nurturing Parent can only interact with another Nurturing Parent or Child (either type).

An Adult can only interact with another Adult.

An Adapted Child can only interact with another Adapted Child or a Parent (either type).

A Natural Child can only interact with another Natural child or a Nurturing Parent.

There needs to be a balance between the two types of parents. A great imbalance will produce either a overbearingly critical parent or a doting, overindulging parent. Listen to the voice within you to hear who dominates. Does that inner voice criticize you or excuse you too lightly? "I am my own worst critic" is a common and accurate phrase. I believe that a primary reason so many Christians seek a savior and forgiveness is because of that inner voice constantly reminding them of their failures. The Critical Parent will not let the Adapted Child feel totally adequate – totally accepted and worthy. Therefore, the child seeks to find that acceptance and forgiveness in God. One step in repentance is the realization that anything said in a negative manner can be said more effectively in a positive manner. A term I learned to use early with my children whenever they misbehaved was, "You are better than that." It clearly communicated the message, but without a derogatory connotation. When you have those inner communications with your Critical Parent, encourage that parent to offer the criticism in a positive, even encouraging way. Sometimes humor is the proper method for responding to some of our failures: "Don't quit your day job," is a term I often humorously tell myself when attempting to perform some task beyond my ability. After that, my Adult may take control and guide me more carefully through the process.

The Adult is our non-emotional, rational self. The Ruler should represent that part in our archetypal selves, incidentally. The Adult does not waste time with blame or guilt. The Adult desires to fix the problem and tries to insure there will be no repeats. The Adult turns the dreams into plans, learns from the past then, and lets it go.

Your Adapted Child has learned how to survive in the world. Your Adapted Child lives with a plethora of *shoulds* and *should nots*. Many of these are good and useful, e.g. brush your teeth, say please and thank you, look both ways before crossing the street. My wife and I once entered the golf course clubhouse just as a group of young men burst through the door at the end of their workday. Their mood was joyful. They were laughing and jostling one another like young teenagers, even though they all appeared to be in the early thirties. My wife observed that fact and commented on it. "You've got it right, hon," I replied. "They've been dutiful men all day, doing all the grown up things they were supposed to do. Now it's time to play, so they are young, carefree boys for the moment." It was a wonderful example of mature, responsible men consciously making the switch from Adapted Child to Natural Child, or in Jungian terms: discarding their Warrior to bring forth their Jester. With absolutely no loss of inner contact these young men merely switched roles. Healthy people do that as a matter of who they are.

Yes, the Natural Child is the one who wants to run barefooted through the park. The Natural Child is sensuous, curious, playful and free-spirited. These are delightful traits, but have their time and their place. When the Natural Child is the Ruler there is trouble ahead.

The model I understand that guides the earnest spiritual pilgrim along our spiritual path is derived from the thinking of Carl Jung. Jung understood humanity as a complex blending of a conscious self and an unconscious Self. As the ego develops and we become mindful of ourselves as a distinct individual with clear boundaries, knowing who we are and who we are not; what we value and what we do not; and what we will stand for and what we will not stand for, this self-aware ego continues to expand to incorporate our unconscious elements that include all our archetypes. The major archetypes tend to unfold in a predictable pattern. First is the Innocent, who lives in Eden and longs to remain there. The longer one resides in Eden, to a point, the more secure the Innocent will be. Erik Erikson refers to the first level of development at that time when a person either develops basic trust or basic distrust – in life – in the world – and in others. A long tenure in Eden develops this basic trust upon which all other attributes will rest.

The Orphan appears when the Innocent is thrust out of Eden. The story of the Fall in Genesis 2 describes this in mythological terms. Adam and Eve eat of the fruit of knowledge. They become self-aware, realizing they are naked, and are cast out of Eden. The Orphan learns to mourn and to become interdependent with others. The Orphan within us is that part of ourselves that responds to such songs as the old spiritual, "Sometimes I feel like a motherless child . . . a long, long way from home." The Orphan is that part that unaccountably sometimes cries at movies or a strand of music. The Orphan carries our sorrow and can relate empathetically to others. The Orphan is also the one who tells us to be careful . . . particularly with strangers.

The Caregiver often appears early in little girls. They play nurse, teacher or mother and give tender care to dolls. Eventually they must learn to also care for themselves or they may transition into Martyrs or simply wear themselves out. Little Boys tend to find their Warrior early. In our society, we may feel concern for those who's Warrior remains inert while the Caregiver or some other less aggressive archetype appears. They often are at least verbally abused and made to feel like outsiders. Names like "nerd" or "sissy" are applied to them. Wise parents will watch to see what the dominant aspects of personality are. Then they will nurture their child's natural gifts. As our culture is changing the stereotypes of old no longer are valid. Girls develop strong warriors and boys become good caregivers. It is no longer unusual to see male nurses and female doctors. We have women serving in the military as generals and admirals. We also have men who choose to be the stay-at-home parent. The Warrior first appears as a young Hero, who is more concerned with the glory than the battle. Heroes must accept every challenge. Mature Warriors learn to choose which battles are important enough to engage in some form of combat. Truly mature Warriors learn to seek win/win situations as the Magician.

At this point I would observe that you must have developed ample trust and learned to care for yourself and to defend yourself (in any number of ways) or you never will travel far on your spiritual journey. You will grow weary or simply be defeated by the struggles you will encounter as you attempt to leave the security of the established way and find your own path. It is good to have someone accompany you on your journey. Bear one another's burdens; share one another's fears, failures and dreams.

Along the way, other archetypes appear. The task for each new arrival is to play its role, which is usually modeled after some personal hero, and then to mature into a natural, assimilated part of the self through the process of Individuation. Personally I believe such hymns as "O Young and Fearless Prophet" should be regular fare for our young people. Stories of Jesus' quiet, non-harmful courage should be well known by them. When we reflect upon our own development we realize that at various times in our lives we modeled ourselves after some admired figure. Jesus should be seen as heroic – for he was. I have observed this modeling, particularly among second lieutenants and new clergypersons. They are not yet comfortable with their new role, so they "play-the-role" for a while. Eventually they develop their true style, one that fits them naturally, thus ending the process of Individuation. If the emerging archetype misbehaves, acting from its libido (Freud) or its elephant (Haidt) the Ruler may decide to exile it into its shadow personality (suppression). These shadow aspects which we try to hide become our troublemakers, creating neuroses and erupting at awkward times.

Suppression does not work. It never has. It never will. Those parts of ourselves we attempt to suppress either will eventually find a way to burst free, without the control of our better selves, or we will wear ourselves down in a state of perpetual depression by the effort of suppressing a vital part of ourselves. A far better process is to claim those seemingly unacceptable dimensions of ourselves and work with them as we would work with a child. Transformation works and is far more rewarding and satisfying. It requires imagination and patience, but it *does* work.

I said I had learned in my early adulthood that people do not tend to become what you tell them to become. Rather, they tend to become what you tell them they *are*. Let's look at that one more time to emphasize the point: I believe the church has made a terrible mistake by calling its people sinners. Imagine, if you will, the effect of parents calling their children losers, lazy, cheaters, liars or some other derisive term. No thoughtful parent would dream of doing such a thing. Those who – because of their own ineptness – have done that have created lasting problems in their children. Why, then, has the Church which purports to be God's representative on earth done this to God's children? This concept of sin was covered in an earlier chapter. I raise this again because I see it as so destructive and demeaning of the human personality. The title, *sinner,* is not one a follower of Jesus should accept or use for others. Jesus told his listeners they were the light of the world, and told them to let their light shine. Paul addressed the churches he wrote as *saints,* or *those called to be saints.* Which dark part of yourself do you believe should be the first to be brought into the light and transformed by love? Which one causes you to wish that aspect of you had remained hidden or at least quiet? We all have some, even though we play peek-a-boo with ourselves, trying to make ourselves believe we are more nearly perfect than we actually are.

As with the first step in the Alcoholics Anonymous Twelve Step Program, the first step for those who would be modern day followers of Jesus is to be totally honest with yourself. No one makes it to adulthood without some injuries – some inner brokenness. What parts of you are broken, distorted or incomplete? Which of those do you believe needs to be tended to first? Ironically, however, it is this shadow community that is one of two pathways leading us into the intimate contact with God. Our shadows lay within the deepest, innermost part of ourselves, and that, as I understand and experience it, is the archway to deity. We are more apt to find God in the valley than on the mountaintop. We are more likely to encounter The One when we call out from our pain and weakness than when we extol our victories and sing our gratitude. The frightened, lonely, injured child within us reaches more fervently for God than any comfortable, secure facet of our personality could imagine. Stripped of any pretense, our cry is that of a parched soul pleading for water. Like Lazarus at the gate we will wait and cry out until we are heard . . . and hear in return: The Trickster who has run out of tricks; the Warrior who deteriorated into a bully; the Magician who crossed into black magic. Any of our potentially worthy attributes that lost the way and was relegated into the shadows finally wearies of her or his misguided and misspent existence. In the desperate starkness of brutal honesty it is these shadow parts of ourselves that stretch just a bit further into our souls to discover the God who has been with us all the time. When we finally tire of the loneliness and emptiness that lies somewhere within us – when we give up trying to pretend we are happier, more successful, more competent and more confident than we know we are, then – and probably only then – will we actually take that critical step at repentance. When we do, our lives will begin to be transformed.

Many years ago, in a best-selling spiritual autobiography,[6] a petroleum engineer named, Keith Miller told of his Damascus Road experience. Keith was successful by the world's standards. He was comfortably married with children. By all overt standards he was living the good life. Yet there was something within him he could not name that kept him from feeling successful. One evening, while in an oil field, Keith stepped out of his car and shouted to the heavens, "God, if there is anything you want of my stinking soul, I give it to you." (cited from memory) Keith said that, although he has no explanation, his life began to work better from that moment. In the course of time, Keith found himself divorced and practicing counseling rather than engineering. His life gradually acquired an entirely new shape. But Keith knew deep within himself that he was becoming the person he believed God made him to be.

The experience of transformation may begin when we discover ourselves sitting alongside Job amidst the ruble of our world and we are most open to hearing the voice of deity calling through our bruised souls . . . or it may begin when we vicariously experience the deep sorrows and longings of others.

A young man, Tom Dooley, had dreams of becoming a successful Park Avenue doctor. He was bright, assertive, self-actualizing, talented and attractive in appearance and personality. He knew he had only to set his sights on a goal to achieve it. While in military service during the Viet Nam War, Tom encountered the Boat People in Laos. They were the displaced refugees of the area who had no place to settle. They lived their lives on small boats with no permanent community. The plight of those people penetrated Tom's soul. Raised in the Catholic Church, Tom had a deep-seated sense of what was

---

6 Miller, Keith, *The Taste of New Wine*, Word Books, Waco, TX, 1965

right and what was wrong - apart from any man-made law. He abandoned all plans for a successful medical career in New York and devoted his life to establishing a network of medical centers for these people who had mysteriously become his own. Tom's story is exceptional, but every year CNN dedicates an evening to honoring similar heroes. Most of us who find our lives changed might do it as we serve volunteer meals, suddenly seeing beyond and beneath the weary faces and ragged clothing of those standing in line. We might feel the gradual change within ourselves as we visit hospital rooms encountering pending deaths to put up new pictures, change flowers or just chat with a lonely stranger. Whenever we place ourselves alongside others in real life situations, striving to offer some degree of assistance or comfort, we are following in the footsteps of the Man of Galilee who promised that a cross was somehow more fulfilling – more satisfying than a crown.

When a cynical reporter asked Dooley what he was getting out of all he was doing, Tom's answer was brief: "Plenty. My life is now worthwhile." That moment was a wonderful example of a spirit-centered person being encountered by someone who probably was a decent person, but was totally incapable of even imagining the truth of what Tom was expressing. *Repentance does mean transformation.*

I read of a very different process of decision making in one of my Myers-Briggs Typological Indicator journals. A young wife, who had never felt to be truly herself, took an MBTI evaluation and was told she was a radically different type than what she believed herself to be. She pondered that information for some time. Then she made a decision to work with a counselor to probe deeply within herself to discover if she was, in fact, this different person. Living the wrong type is more common than it should be. It usually is the result of an overly strict parent insisting the child emulates one or the other parent. The child conforms and adapts, but never feels *genuine*. In the process, her husband told her he did not like who she was becoming and told her to stop the process. However, by this time the young lady was certain she was finally discovering and experiencing her true self. No threat or enticement was going to change her. Her husband divorced her. She entered a profession that was consistent with her newly found personality. I had to contact her to learn more. She was comfortable and content with herself for the first time in her life.

As we spoke I recalled the words of Jesus saying that unless one could "hate his family" (Jesus often used hyperbole) one could not enter the Kingdom. I have witnessed the need for many persons to "hate their family" – to stop being either the symptom bearers for the family illness or the figment of their imagination – in order to become whole and healed.

So there are three examples of fine persons who found different paths to their personal repentance. Tom's was sudden and radically life changing. Keith's was gradual, both in a decision to change and in the process of transformation. The young lady responded to a deep-seated inner conflict that drove her to intentionally make a radical transformation toward wholeness.

A final, quite dramatic transformation: in 1961 I met a young African American pastor. We both were new to the ministry and still trying to learn what that actually meant. He was friendly, spoke in a pleasant tenor-quality voice, and enjoyed entertaining us with humorous anecdotes. I did not encounter him again for about eight years. Martin Luther King Jr. had been assassinated, as had Bobby Kennedy. The Civil Rights Movement had gathered momentum and was erupting everywhere. When the minister entered the room I was stunned. He was the speaker we had assembled to hear tell us of the progress of the Civil Rights Movement locally. He had not grown an inch, but somehow he appeared larger – he occupied more space. His mere presence projected a sense of power. When he spoke it was with a voice a full octave lower than what I remembered. It resonated with authority. This time there were no humorous anecdotes designed to please. This time he spoke calmly and directly to us about the injustice that had held us all in captivity for far too many generations. When he finished, I reflected on the biblical statement: "He spoke as one with authority."

Later I pondered what had caused the dramatic change – this dramatic metamorphosis of personality – I had witnessed. I realized that there is far more to this quality of humanness than I ever imagined. Somewhere – somehow – this compliant young man had found his soul – his genuine Self. He had discarded the friendly mask most of us wear and began to be the person God had intended him to be, realizing the power that resides in each of us. He was now a genuine follower of the Man from Galilee who gave his life revealing what genuine justice truly means. I still marvel at the transformation of this one, simple person who became a genuine leader in one of our most significant struggles for justice.

Points to Ponder

There are various models you can use for understanding the workings of your inner self. They are just that: models. I have presented some that you may find helpful. Ultimately each of us is solely responsible for our own lives for we are the ones who must live them. Whatever blame we might like to pass along to others is a waste of time and energy. The more honestly we explore our inner selves the more likely we are to make better, healthier decisions that will result in better, healthier relationships and activities.

Time spent in reflective, dialogical prayer is time well spent. Talk with your Critical Parent and help her learn to present the criticisms in a positive manner. Criticism can and should be helpful – not hurtful. Look for those frightened, broken parts of you and let them know they are loved and precious – even though misbehaving. Without loading yourself with guilt, try to understand where and how things went bad in some of the relationships.

Finally, did you feel a bit edgy as you read some of these tales of transformation? What if God were to transform you in a similar manner? How far do you want to travel to be a genuine follower of the Man of Galilee?

Chapter Twenty

A Jungian Model for the Spiritual Journey

I had previously stated that when I first encountered the works of Carl Jung I believed I saw where it offered an intellectual framework and method for the Western mind to pursue a spiritual path. What I write is a blending of my interpretation of Jung's work with my evolving theology.

Carl Jung perceived humans as being a combination of two selves: one conscious and the other unconscious. As the ego enlarges to incorporate our unconscious human potential the spiritual pilgrim has the opportunity to communicate more fully with his unconscious Self. This unconscious Self is larger and wiser than our conscious. It never sleeps for it has no need to sleep. It has no ego issues to distract it or distort its perception. However, it has a language all its own. Our unconscious expresses itself in symbols. These symbols tend to be those that have formed the basis for various mythologies throughout time. It was in interpreting clients' dreams that Jung first became aware of this. Clients with no knowledge of ancient mythologies spoke of the figures in their dreams as some of those ancient mythological figures, performing in the same manner as the myths. This caused him to postulate a collective unconscious that was common to all humans. These ancient symbols and many more which were discovered to be common symbols of the unconscious, form the language by which our conscious minds must interact with the unconscious Self that resides within us all. When at the Jungian

Institute in Zurich, I innocently asked why our unconscious could not speak English, because it would have made communication so much easier. My question was met with a question: "Why don't we Swiss speak English so you could understand us better, as well?"

I offer that in case the question had also crossed your mind.

Jung believed that in every male person a female soul or *anima* quietly resided, and in every female a male soul or *animus*, also quietly resided. The more secure we are in our sexuality the more we accept this inner soul and are willing to communicate with it. This is entirely an unconscious decision, but it does have conscious repercussions. Those who are unsure or uncomfortable with their sexuality may repress the quiet soul within them. Consequently, when they encounter that quality in their conscious self they may react with anger – which always is a reaction to a perceived threat. This is the reason the super macho male often is the one who reacts most strongly against homosexuality and is likely to be more aggressive with females. Most of us will learn from our inner souls and over a lifetime find ourselves to be more androgynous in our later years.[7]

In this regard I must point out that Jung believed the attractive person of the opposite sex you encounter in your dream is your counter-sexual soul. As you develop a relationship with her/him be careful not to allow yourself to become seduced. You are to make friends with that other self – not lovers.

One rather common dream phenomenon is the appearance of a person we have known and thought of as wise. This usually occurs sometime early in midlife. It is the Sage quality making an appearance in our dream to inform us that he or she is now available to us. Wisdom accumulates over the years. A young person may be very intelligent, but totally lacking in wisdom. An older person of normal mental capability may be among the wisest we know. Many times you retire at night, still pondering a problem, but you arise with

7 In the Creation Story in Genesis 1 God says, "Let us make humanity in our image. Male and female God created them." God is neither male nor female as we think of those qualities, but if we are in God's image each of us possesses both qualities.

the problem solved. That unsleeping Sage within has worked on it and quietly informed you while you slept.

Such it is with many of those unconscious parts of you. Ever so slowly they rise into your consciousness, gradually becoming assimilated into your merging total personality. If they are guided and shaped by whoever is in charge of your conscious personality as a follower of Jesus, this final person will have experienced a gradual metamorphosis. Somewhere in the process, the ego cedes to the inner Self, which Jung also called *The Image of God.* Some will exclaim they have been born again, and this time they will be correct. Others may simply experience a profound sense of wellbeing and energy. Their lives will be focused. Their value system will have altered dramatically.

Few of us will make this complete transition in this lifetime. That, for me is part of our eternal quest. Also, whenever I write or speak on this subject I am tempted to cite Paul; "Do not think that I have achieved this yet, or that I have taken hold of it." (Philippians 3:12)

It is time now to return to an earlier thought: what is the source of the thoughts that rise within us, and the words that flow so naturally to express our thoughts? A computer may be turned on and ready to exceed our mental skills the moment we ask it to do so. However, until we prod it, the computer is inert – mindless, with no awareness of the passage of time. Most of us have had the experience of not fully understanding what we are thinking until we have put it into words. We also have had the experience of having our minds search around for the proper words, then recognizing the right ones as they appear even before we have clearly expressed the thought to ourselves. It is so natural that we rarely, if ever, wonder about it. Yet this source is the key to our humanity. This is why Rene' Descartes could say, "I think therefore I am." It is the reason so-called artificial intelligence can never fully replace the human mind. It can do the chores that human intelligence tells it to do, but it can never conceptualize the totally new. It cannot want or desire, or feel deep remorse. These qualities belong to a realm that we can neither duplicate nor create: the *human soul.* This is the divine quality that resides in each person, to which the Hindus refer with the term of greeting: *Namaste,* the ancient Stoics called *Logoi*, and Paul called *"Christ within me."*

Becoming familiar with this dimension of yourself is the fist step in your journey. Scripture is essential. However, you must read it as a guidebook, not a legal document. I suggest you begin with the Gospel accounts. Mark is the oldest and purest. Start with Mark. Ask yourself who this Jesus of Nazareth is. Do not be influenced by old Sunday school teachings learned as a child. I would suggest Marcus Borg's *Meeting Jesus Again for the First Time,* [8] as a good resource, even before you open Mark. It is an excellent means for clearing the mind of old, often-false beliefs. Read the letters attributed to Peter and John. They express the understandings of the faith in its infancy. When you read Paul's letters, remember that they were personal notes to specific people, dealing with specific issues of their time. Skip the letter to Timothy and the Book of Revelation. They will only confuse you. Paul did not write those letters. They reveal a much later development of the church. John the beloved disciple is not John of Patmos. His description of God is abhorrent. It is embraces and glorifies the desire for revenge that resides in too many hearts. In my opinion any literal interpretation of the Book of Revelation is pure, destructive heresy.

Scripture is the place to begin. It is the prelude to the journey. It is not the journey anymore than studying a map or reading travelogues is the journey. An actual journey requires movement and change of some sort. I highly recommend a daily time of meditation. This clears and calms the mind and helps one move more deeply into one's inner Self. Mental and even physical help professionals now are recommending meditation as a part of daily practice. They claim it reduces stress and serves to create a healthier, happier and longer life. It can't hurt so why not give it a try? Begin with short terms of meditation: 5-7 minutes. As you grow comfortable with the experience you will naturally increase the duration until you find that time frame that is right for you. Fifteen minutes is comfortable for me. I got out of the habit of evening meditation, but find that when I do evening meditation I sleep better and arise with greater energy and clarity.

As the process of meditation becomes a natural part of your daily routine you will discover yourself being a bit calmer and feeling more possessed of wisdom. That is because you have allowed yourself to enter into more direct communication with your unconscious self that is a part of your soul. By soul

---

8 Borg, Marcus, *Meeting Jesus for the First Time, New York: Harper Collins Publishers, 1994*

I simply mean the quality of being that you are at your core. It is that portion of your being that is eternal that moves ever closer to becoming the image of God in which you were created. We do not retain all of the memories and acquired skills and understandings of our lifetimes, *but we do remain what we have become.*

There, I have said it: our journey is endless – eternal. But my endless journey is not the travels of Richard Cheatham, American male. It is the journey of one made in the image of God to grow and become a companion of God. I have no idea what that looks like. I only believe it is true and I base my life's actions on that belief. I believe it because it is the only understanding of eternal life that makes sense to me. I believe it because it is consistent with everything I know and believe about Jesus of Nazareth and the God he revealed. To become his follower requires us to live intentionally in such a way that we become Christ-like – or as Christ-like as we are able in this lifetime. Getting a passing grade so we can make it to live happily in heaven for eternity makes absolutely no sense. This notion arises from our egocentricity and need to feel both secure and special.

When Jesus speaks of storing up treasures in heaven rather than upon earth (Matthew 6:20) try interpreting it in terms of this understanding. Then try making sense of it in the traditional understanding of residing in a place of eternal bliss. When he presents us with a loving God who continually forgives us, try interpreting that in the light of heaven or hell decision after a few brief years on earth. In an unimaginably mammoth universe consisting of billions of galaxies there must be many other planets with intelligent life – some probably millions or billions of years more advanced than we. The Garden of Eden myth no longer can be understood in any literal sense in such a universe – nor can the Exodus or Flood. The God revealed through Jesus Christ does not seek punishment nor forget about any of his children. This God revealed by Jesus Christ empowers and moves His creations toward fulfillment, and has an eternity to complete His plans. So: "Hang on!" There is no short-term program that transforms the faithful in an eight-week course. There is a gradually acquired lifestyle that sets the course for spiritual health in much the same way that a physically healthy lifestyle can cause you to extend your vitality, agility and general health.

Chapter Twenty-One

Worshiping as You Journey

There are two Greek terms that we translate as "I worship." One is *proskune'o*. The other is *latreu'o*. They represent different dynamics. Both are essential elements of genuine worship. Technically, the first means to prostrate oneself as in total obedience, much as the Muslims do in their time of prayer. The second means to work for, or to serve. I found that in some translations the term *latreu'o* is translated, apparently indiscriminately, as either *worship* or *service.*

There was a great hymn in a former Methodist hymnal. They claim it was discarded because of sexist language. I believe a touch of imagination could have remedied that. I fear it was discarded because the church lost its focus. The second verse of "O Brother Man" reads like this:

> For he whom Jesus loved has truly spoken
> The holier worship which he deigns to bless
> Restores the lost and binds the spirit broken
> And feeds the widow and the fatherless.

If the church still had that principle of service as its primary focus there might be fuller worship services today. Service to those in need is an absolute minimum level of participation for any follower of Jesus – in any culture – at any time in history.

The other question of how we should worship in the manner conducive to spiritual growth is at one level simple, but requires more explanation.

Since I used a hymn to justify my first thought I will offer another for this:

> Take time to be holy, speak oft with thy Lord.
> Abide with him always, and dwell on his word.
> Make friends of God's children. Help those who are weak.
> Forgetting in nothing his blessings to seek.

We need a means for consciously placing ourselves in the presence of God. As for which church one should attend, I find that the sign on the door means very little today. It might give you a hint as to the style of liturgy and the selection of hymns. However, the underlying theological premises that guide the sermon and the entire service usually vary with the person standing in the pulpit. Even the theology is not as important as the experience of the preacher. I have heard sermons that run against the grain of my theology. However, I am aware there is no one correct theology. There never has been; there never will be. What we have are an endless variety of intellectual pathways that offer a way to enter into a loving, empowering, liberating relationship with God. When I sense preachers who actually have found their path I set aside my theological tools and let the them tell me their story. "By your fruits you are known," is the phase I learned, not "by the fertilizer that has been spread upon you." On the opposite side, I have been to churches where the hymns and liturgy are comfortably familiar. The words coming from the pulpit seem reasonably consistent with my own thinking. Still I cannot wait for them to end. The words just did not ring true. The illustrations seemed like the ones found on the Internet and there was a lack of personal conviction in the preacher's voice and manner. Finely crafted phrases cannot replace depth and sincerity.

So find a church where the sermon rings true of a relationship with God. Find one where the sermons address the issues of your life, and make no assumption that you are spiritually whole and ready to go forth. If the theology is different, reconcile it on the way home. If no church is available that offers these basics then seek or start a group who will gather for study, prayer, fellowship and service as followers of this man of Galilee known as Jesus.

Find a gathering of common spirits. Our faith cannot grow in a vacuum, nor can it thrive in a sterile setting. Ministers come and go, but congregations tend to persevere and provide stability in our lives. Small groups provide the stuff for genuine spiritual growth over the years. In the give and take of small, social groups we learn to care for even members with whom we may have little in common. We learn to understand and live with differences. We learn the differing perspectives and expressions of a faith we share. We learn that people are more important than narrow expressions of that faith.

I am a part of some organizations where most of the others have very different personal histories from mine. We have different faiths or expressions of faith. We share few common experiences and interests, so we would rarely, if ever, socialize. Yet I am extremely fond of so many of them. What we do together matters. It really matters. We help to heal relationships and broken lives. We search for the commonality that lies beneath the surface of us all. In searching we find more along the way and feel more tightly bound as a result. In short, our service creates community – real community – not the "Good to see you," "How's it going?", "See you next week" variety of community, but, something more than that.

Some worship opportunities are not planned or scheduled. They simply burst forth. They may happen in a crowd, a small group or in solitude. Occasionally I have encountered sunrises or sunsets that are overwhelmingly sacred in their glory and magnitude. They require that I stop whatever I am doing and give full attention to what God is doing in that moment. Sometimes I am allowed to witness a scene of tenderness between two persons that causes me to hold my breath and just share in the wonder of being human. Sometimes in the midst of activity some flash of insight or radically different perspective passes through my mind, and for that brief instant a sense of awe or marvel tingles within me. We live in an unexplainable mystery whose wonder has an endless variety of ways of revealing itself. Each of these moments is for me a moment of worship. They are brief acknowledgements of "How Great Thou Art" experiences.

Look for them and celebrate them as you move through your days. There is no need to wait for Sunday, for the organ to begin, or for someone to place an order of worship in your hand. Let your heart develop sacred eyes and sacred ears to help you experience the wonder in which we live . . . constantly!

Paul called us to *pray* without ceasing. He could have easily substituted the word *worship.*

Chapter Twenty-Two

Summary and Reminders

So where do we find ourselves at this point?

If you have been thinking theologically alongside me you have recognized that we Christians have never had one unified expression of our faith. The four Gospel writers had different understandings of the nature of Jesus that ranged from a spirit-filled person to the incarnation of the divine will and nature of God. Later theologians went so far as to believe Jesus actually was God in the flesh. You learned that people shaped their religious beliefs with the understanding of their specific cultures. As a result, the different expressions grew in distinctly different directions. You should have observed that each of those differing interpretations offered valid means for developing a relationship with the living God. Each within the context of their culture made sense to the believers, and offered renewal.

You also realize that Jesus always pointed to a deity who was greater than he was. He never offered an explanation of the purpose his death. He never told his followers to be good. He invited them to live in the Kingdom of God but never promised them an eternity in a bliss-filled heaven. He never suggested life would be easy or prosperous if they followed him, but invited them to take up their crosses and follow him anyway. He bitterly opposed the religious legalism of his time, and told the people if they continued to follow him they would learn a truth that would set them free.

You learned that the world of the first century writers does not begin to compare with the world in which you live. That first century world had the

Earth at the center, and was circled by the Sun. The planets and stars served as a heavenly canopy. When people wished to commune with God they climbed a mountain that brought them perceptively closer to their God. Your world extends almost fourteen billion light years and is rapidly expanding. Within your world there are countless billions of galaxies containing millions of suns, each with its own solar system. The thought of a physical heaven – or deity residing within that heaven - amid this makes no rational sense.

The deity presented in the books of the old covenant ranges from a simple human-like deity who molds a man out of clay, to a much greater deity who pronounces light and in the pronouncing, actually creates that light. That deity ranges from a human-like deity who forgets about his children, Israel, to one who knows what is to be, long before it happens. He ranges from one who is loving and forgiving, to one who is vengeful and jealous. Whereas, if you omit the Book of Revelation, the deity presented in the books of the new covenant is loving, forgiving, redemptive, and empowering. Hopefully you have figured out that the books of the old and new covenant reveal the history of humanity's search to understand God. The steady progression from a tribal deity to the one creator God of all humanity is slowly revealed. The tribal names eventually blend into one, YHWH. In the final writings of the unknown prophet of the Exile we find in Isaiah 40-66 (circa 350 B.C.E.) we read these first proclamations of radical monotheism:

> *Thus says the Lord, the creator of the heavens, he who is God, who made the earth and fashioned it, and himself fixed it fast, who created it no empty void but made it a place to dwell therein. I am the Lord. There is no other.* (Isaiah 45:18)

> *It is too slight a task for you as my servant to restore the tribes of Jacob, to bring back the descendants of Israel: I will make you a light to the nations, to be my salvation to the earth's farthest bounds.* (Isaiah 49:6)

In the scope of about 1500 years the small, tribal deity of a nomadic colony had grown in the minds of faithful followers to become the all-powerful creator, redeemer God of all the earth. Legalism and egocentricity combined to make this deity a legalistic, judgmental and punitive deity, until Jesus presented a greater step forward with God as a loving, redeeming, empowering God of us all. The same dynamics of egocentricity and legalism once more have transformed that version of God into a moralistic, legalist, confining and judgmental deity in the minds of many. It is that deity from whom the younger generations are fleeing. While it is the loving, Father-God of Jesus for whom they (and we) are silently hungering.

I hope that you have learned to distinguish between what I call Presence and Spirit. We continually live in God's Presence. The Psalmist understood this:

> *Where can I escape from your spirit?*
> *Where can I flee from your presence?* (Psalm 139:7)

For him, presence and spirit were synonymous. He was pre-Hellenistic. His God was the Hebrew God who dwelt with His people. Also, he, as is true with many poets, was sensitive to that ongoing presence in his life that was both a part *of* him and apart *from* him. Spirit is the term for the awakened divine portion within you. It is what Paul described as "Christ within me," because he could not possibly imagine himself to be possessed of the divine. It is what many today call the spirit at work within them. It is the source of fresh energy and insight that can propel a person beyond the ordinary. We see it all the time . . . in others but are afraid to acknowledge it within ourselves. To do so might radically change our lives.

You have had the opportunity of reviewing most of our faith's great, traditional teachings as seen from the paradigm of the 4th century and from the 21st century. Some of you embraced the new perspectives eagerly. Some of you are more cautious about doing so. That is not as critical as your rethinking the principle teachings about sin, redemption and salvation. The new paradigm does not find these to be of value – if they ever really were. God's acceptance and empowerment - and call to be in fellowship with Him in this life and beyond is the biblical message, and the message of the first century church. That is what we wish to reclaim and proclaim.

The early church buildings had no pews. They were gathering places for those who had been called out (*ecclesia*) to be the body of Christ, still proclaiming his message of our heavenly Father's love, acceptance and eternal plan for his children. They went into the world, caring for those in need, offering open arms to strangers, forgiving the brutality, betrayals and bigotry of the ignorant, self-centered masses. Their impact on an uncaring culture was so powerful that Paul could write:

> *What I mean is that God was in Christ reconciling the world*
> *to himself, no longer holding humanity's sins against them,*
> *and that he has entrusted us with the message of reconciliation.*
> (2 Corinthians 5:19)

Too many of us who bear the name of Christian have lost that understanding of our faith. This is the reason for the dramatic decline of Christianity in our time. Far too many who bear his name spend their time reading and citing Scripture. They believe they know a great deal *about* the Man of Nazareth. Perhaps they do, at least as he has been defined by scholars and non-scholars through the centuries. However, there is only one way that anyone takes the step from knowing *about* to actually *knowing* a person.

In the early part of the last century, there lived a man named Albert Schweitzer. He was a German theologian/musician of extraordinary talent. As a church organist he was world-renowned for his interpretation of Bach. As a theologian he wrote the monumental work: *The Quest for the Historical Jesus.*[9] In it, Albert Schweitzer proclaimed that the man, Jesus, had been so covered by legend and myth and viewed through the eyes of those with apocalyptic expectations that it was impossible to find him through the words of Scripture. I shall never forget his ending summary:

> *He comes to us as one unknown, without a name, as of old, by the lakeside; he came to those men who knew him not. He speaks to us the same words:*

---

9 Albert Schweitzer, *The Quest for the Historic Jesus,* trans. W. Montgomery, London, A. and C. Black, 1911

> *"Follow thou me," and sets us to the task he has to fulfill in our time. He commands, and to those who obey him, whether they be wise or simple, he will reveal himself in the toils, the conflicts, the sufferings which they shall pass through in his fellowship. And – as in an ineffable mystery, they shall learn in their own experience, who he is.*

Essentially Albert Schweitzer realized that the force that gave rise to this movement we call Christianity was not so much the Jesus of history, but the Risen Christ of eternity. It was the Risen Christ who promised to be with us forever. It was the Risen Christ who breathed his spirit into his followers. Later, while touring Africa, Schweitzer had his Pauline Damascus Road experience – his Tom Dooley Boat People experience. He came across hippopotami bathing in the river. Rather than merely seeing these huge, absurd-looking creatures and wishing to photograph them, Schweitzer had a moment of divine insight: *"Reverence for life,"* flashed across his mind as he gazed at them. Albert returned to Germany, resigned his chair at the university, went to medical school, and returned to Africa where he spent the remainder of his life as a medical missionary.

Once we begin our journey of following – not the historic Jesus - but the *Risen Christ* we no longer chart our own course. Years ago, a young Baptist preacher who had just earned his PhD was offered a teaching position at a prestigious seminary in the suburbs of Chicago. His letter of response expressed gratitude for the offer but stated that he felt called to the parish ministry at that time. Usually someone with a hard-earned PhD would jump at such an opportunity, but this young man's goals were not dictated by his personal ambition. His decision kept a small group of seminarians from benefitting from his knowledge, but it gave the world a leader at a critical time in history: Dr. Martin Luther King Jr. [10]

Our Christian heritage is filled with those faithful who placed obedience to God above their personal interest or safety. Few stand out in history. Most were just one more face in the crowd – one more voice crying in the wilderness. However, it has been those lost faces and voices that kept this faith alive and vital. It was the mother of three who decided to adopt the

---

10 Dr. King's letter was only recently discovered in the archives of Garrett Evangelical Theological Seminary in Evanston, IL

child or children around her who did not seem to have parents who loved or nurtured them. It was the teacher who toiled in poverty-stricken areas to give the children some chance at life. It was the clerk who volunteered as a scout leader or evening tutor, the activist who spoke out at assemblies, the doctor who volunteered for missionary work, the retiree who volunteered at the hospital or schools to do what was needed, or it may have been any number of people who determined that their lives were meant to be lived in such a way as to make this world a better place. Perhaps they had a vision of God's plan for them. Perhaps they just were enough "in touch" with God's Presence to respond to the cries of humanity.

A few final stories: a middle school football team in Olivet, Michigan had befriended a young, academically challenged teammate. This was a middle school, mind you. The students are at that age when their hormones are beginning to rage, and there often is a lot of cruelty and recklessness running loose. Yet, these young men conspired to surprise him, their coaches – and the entire student body by doing something that far exceeded the term *nice*. Late in a game they were certain they would win, one of the players ran the ball to the one-yard line – and stopped there, downing the ball. They called a time out and brought their young friend into the huddle. He was to carry the ball on the next play. The play is recorded on video and can be seen on the Internet, but you will not see the young ball carrier. You will only see a protective gang of young men moving across the goal line and bursting forth in joyful celebration. Anyone who has ever played football remembers his first touchdown. It is like your first kiss, your first sweetheart, your first car! It is something *you never forget*!

They had conspired to give him this gift of a lifetime. A group of young middle school boys teamed up to give a gift of healing, redemptive love. The young boy who carried that ball, now would be looked upon differently by the entire student body. He had been embraced and endorsed by their entire football team. Once he had been nobody. Now he was somebody special.

The real point of my sharing this however is what occurred during an interview with one of the boys from the team. He was a good-looking young man, obviously athletic and self-assured. He expressed how pleased he had been with what the team did. Then he admitted he never would have thought of it. He was wrapped up in himself, as most people of that age. Then he expressed the joy he had felt in being a part of that. A door within him had opened up, and he really did not recognize that. He just knew he wanted to have that experience again and again. For me, it did not matter what faith, if any, he professed. A profound repentance had begun within him. Without realizing the profundity of what had occurred, this young man had moved – a long way - from pure egocentricity toward theocentricity. He now found greater joy in doing for others than in doing for himself. Oh, yes, he will revert many times on his journey. We all do that. Still, he has tasted from the chalice – and the taste was good. It was compelling enough that he will return time and time again.

In another instance I was wandering through the atrium of our church after a Sunday worship in February, and I saw a friend sitting at a table that had held a sign displaying just one word: *Epiphany*. Epiphany is January 6th, so I suggested that she either missed something or was starting awfully early. She explained that Epiphany was a ministry, similar to the Emmaus Walk that was conducted for the young men who were incarcerated at the Cyndi Taylor Krier Detention Center in the south part of town. I paused to digest this and realized I had done the "hungry and fed, sick and visited, stranger and welcomed – really all of those – but not the "prison and visited." (Matthew 25:31-41) "Perhaps," I thought, "it is time for me to do that, as well."

So I signed up – and shall forever be grateful that I did.

By the end of the first program I was hooked. One young man stood to share his experience: "I had pretty well given up on people," he said. "All they did was use me, lie to me, steal from me or cheat me in some way." Then he paused, looked around at us and continued – with strong but controlled emotion: "But I have never been in a room with so many good people." At every Epiphany session I see young men who if they had been raised in a different family probably would not be there. They would be honor students, involved in school activities, heading for college. I also see some I believe might be beyond our reach at the moment, but there are the others – so many others – who are genuinely searching, struggling to find a better path – a better way of life. There are two weekends per year. Then we meet once a month for five months after the weekend, and we get to observe their progress. Every now and then I realize that I am some small part of helping some young man change his life and find a better way. Then I have something of the feeling of that young middle school athlete. "This is good. I am so pleased- so honored – to be a part of this young man's life."

This eighty plus year-old body had trouble keeping up with the routine. It is an intensive weekend experience. There are two short nights when I will be fortunate to get six hours sleep. I finally learned to take an energy drink to keep from snoozing during some of the afternoon talks. Still, by the end of the three-day weekend I am exhausted. Yet – all-in-all - I do not want to miss being there. I am so grateful that I wandered over to Sarah's table that Sunday morning. It has added more meaning – more joy - to my life.

Years ago I heard a tale about a tiny village in the Alps, where mountain climbing was held in high esteem. The villagers treated the best climbers like Olympic champions. If someone died in a climbing accident the words, "He died climbing" were inscribed on his headstone. It was a high tribute – a final word of adulation to a fallen hero. I realize that I am well past the time in life to scale the heights of my profession or any of my significant avocations. Frankly I am past the time when I believe any additional honors are of genuine value. Yet there is some part of me that responds to those words, "He died climbing." When I consider the days that may still lay ahead I am made conscious of the Hindu concept of the mountain we all are called to climb. We start in various places, so we necessarily will take different paths. Still, it is the same mountain we all seek to climb. As we meet others along the way we are not to criticize them for being on a path different from our own. If anything, we might chat with them and learn something of their path and their journey. It may assist us in finding our way and traversing difficult terrain. We can encourage one another and even reach over to assist another as we travel. It's not a competitive event. When anyone – on any path - scales that final peak and reaches the top, it should be enough to make us all cheer.

I don't want it carved in stone, but I would like to believe that when I have taken that final step I will know that somewhere someone will smile and think, "He died climbing." There are crosses lying around that need carrying. Find the one – that burden of society – that you feel called to bear. Place it as comfortably as you can on your shoulders, for the journey is a long one. Then look for the footprints of the One who called you by name, and start following. The path moves upward!

Selected Bibliography

Armstrong, Karen. *A History of God*: The 4,000-year Quest of Judaism, Christianity and Islam, New York: Ballantine Books, 1993

Berne, Eric, *Games People Play*, New York: Ballantine Books,1964

Borg, Marcus, *Meeting Jesus Again for the First Time*, New York: Harper Collins, 1995

Borg, Marcus, *The Heart of Christianity: Recovering a Life of Faith,* San Francisco: Harper Collins, 2004

Brown, Peter, *Augustine of Hip*po, London: Faber & Faber, 1976

Caldwell, Nigel, *Einstein's Universe,* New York: Bantam Books, 1974

Chadwick, Henry. *The Early Church*. Revised edition Vol 1, Penguin History of the Church, London: Penguin Books, 1993

Gottwald, Norman*, Light to the Nations,* New York: Harper, 1959

Haidt, Jonathan*, The Happiness Hypothesis: Finding Modern Truth in Ancient Wisdom*, New York: Basic Books, 2006

Hawking, Stephen*, A Brief History of Time*, New York: Bantam Books, 1998

Keller, Werner, *The Bible as History: A Confirmation of the Book of books*, trans. William Neil, New York: William Morrow and Company, 1959

Kurtz, Paul, *Science and Religion*, Amherst, New York: Prometheus Books, 2003

Kushner, Harold, *When Bad Things Happen to Good People*, New York: Anchor Books, 1981

Miller, Keith, *The Taste of New Wine*, Waco, TX: Word Books, 1965

Nicolson, Iain, *Dark Side of the Universe: Dark Matter Dark energy, and the Fate of the Universe*, Baltimore: John Hopkins University Press , 2007

Pagels, Elaine, Beyond Belief: The Secret Gospel of Thomas, New York: Vintage Books, 2003

Pearson, Carol, *Awakening the Hero Within*, San Francisco: Harper, 1991

Schweitzer, Albert, *The Quest for the Historic Jesus*, trans. W. Montgomery, London: A and C Black, 1911

Stevens, Anthony, *Archetypes: A Natural History of the Self,* New York: Quill, 1983

About the Author

A life-long Methodist, Richard Cheatham finally awoke to the reality and relevance of God and Jesus in his early twenties. Since then, he has been on a personal quest to discover and recover the qualities of the early followers of Jesus Christ He served as an artillery officer in the Korean War. He left the family boat business to enter the ministry at age thirty-one. He was designated a Wells Scholar and awarded the National Preaching Fellowship of the Methodist Church in his M.Div. and doctoral studies at Garrett Theological Seminary and Northwestern University. His doctoral emphasis was the Patristic era and the Reformation. He studied both koine (biblical) and classical Greek and uses that skill to research early documents and to properly interpret some faulty translations of Scripture. His honors concentration was in psychology, and he did post-doctoral work at the Jungian Institute in Zurich, Switzerland. He has taught World Religions at the university level, and has served as a guest lecturer on critical thinking for the University of Michigan. He is a member of the Association of Psychological Type. Dr. Cheatham served seven very different congregations over a fifty-year period. While serving these congregations he also served as an adjunct professor at various seminaries and colleges. He is the author of three other books: *Can You Make the Buttons Even?, The God Makers, and The Pilgrim Messiah.* He is married to Diane, the father of three daughters, Deborah, Cynthia and Crystal, and the grandfather of seven grandchildren – all gifted and talented beyond belief.

30515958R00122

Made in the USA
Charleston, SC
18 June 2014